You're Making Me Hate You

ALSO BY COREY TAYLOR

*Seven Deadly Sins: Settling the Argument Between
Born Bad and Damaged Good*

*A Funny Thing Happened on the Way to Heaven:
Or, How I Made Peace with the Paranormal and
Stigmatized Zealots and Cynics in the Process*

You're Making Me Hate You

A Cantankerous Look
At The Common Misconception
That Humans Have Any
Common Sense Left

Corey Taylor

Da Capo Press
A Member of the Perseus Books Group

Photos by Strati Hovartos

Designed by Jack Lenzo
Set in 11 point Warnock by The Perseus Books Group

Cataloging-in-Publication data for this book is available from the Library of
Congress.
First Da Capo Press edition 2015
ISBN: 978-0-306-82358-9
ISBN: 978-0-306-82359-6 (e-book)

Published by Da Capo Press
A Member of the Perseus Books Group
www.dacapopress.com

Da Capo Press books are available at special discounts for bulk purchases
in the U.S. by corporations, institutions, and other organizations. For more
information, please contact the Special Markets Department at the Perseus
Books Group, 2300 Chestnut Street, Suite 200, Philadelphia, PA 19103, or call
(800) 810-4145, ext. 5000, or e-mail special.markets@perseusbooks.com.

10 9 8 7 6 5 4 3 2

To Ryan and Griffin, Haven and Lawson, Angeline and Aravis . . .
I love you all with the whole of my heart . . .
I only hope you grow to be better than me.

—CT

The difference between stupidity and genius is that genius has its limits.

—Albert Einstein

I have tried to know absolutely nothing about a
great many things,
and I have succeeded fairly well.

—Robert Benchley

Hell is other people.

—Jean-Paul Sartre, *No Exit*

Which one of these words don't you understand?
Talking to you is like clapping with one hand!

—Anthrax, "Caught in a Mosh," *Among the Living*

CONTENTS

CHAPTER 1

JUST BEFORE THE STORM

Foreboding fake disclaimer: By reading this book and subsequently promoting its contents, whether in physical conversation or digital form, you are entering into an informal contractual congress with the author, one Corey Taylor, known from here on out as "The Neck." This verbal agreement, semilegally recognized in several states and countries (including Guam), gives The Neck permission to smack any of you readers in the face with a plastic wiffle ball bat if and when you commit any of the ridiculously idiotic atrocities that will eventually be described in the tome you now hold in your hands. Herein there will be no warnings or recognition of first offenses regarding violation of this so-called dumbass agreement, and the resulting punishment will most likely happen when you least expect it, coming at the author's earliest convenience, depending on his amateur squash league schedule and other proclivities. If these terms do not appeal to "the better angels" of your judgment, you are encouraged to cease reading this book immediately or, better

1

yet, pass it on to someone you are convinced will be susceptible to
breaking this covenant, thus setting the stage for retribution. You
will then be enlisted to assist The Neck in finding the offender's
residence, affording you a front-row seat to watch the plastic vio-
lence firsthand. Thank you.

It was a weird, drunken, spooky night twelve years ago.

I'd love to say I remember it well, but the fact of the matter
is my old friend Jack Daniels and I had engaged in a battle of
wills that night. Jack won; I placed. So what I can muster from
my shitty college dorm room called a memory bank is fuzzy, at
least for the first half of the proceedings. Through nobody's fault
but my own, shit happened all down my leg. That is as close to
foreshadowing as I am going to go at this point because what I
do recall is precariously close to the sort of thing you hear about
when someone sits you down for a cautionary tale about drugs
and booze and bullshit. So pretend for a moment that I am the
parent and you are the child. I think it goes without saying that
you're snickering, and the paltry attempts to stave off that snickering is not appreciated, but I get it. It is indeed a strain to imagine yours truly as the voice of reason. After all, I'm the guy who
stuck his dick in an orange at a meet-and-greet for $26.10 . . . in
change. Please just bear with me if you can bear the tension. I
promise the following story will not only set the stage for this
book in rare form but will also hopefully make you chuckle,
chortle, and snort as well. God forbid, you might even learn
something. I highly doubt that last prediction.

If you've read any of my other tomes of torment, you will naturally understand that twelve years ago was my notorious epic
run during the making of *Vol. 3: The Subliminal Verses*. Honestly, I could milk that period of my life for as long as I punch
pain into inputs, but this book is much more about the present
and the future. So I am only going to dip into this particular

ink well for a brief moment because it has some insight into the topic at hand. It involves alcohol, various nefarious drugs, a party, a redhead, and a man in an ill-fitting bandana wearing leather pants. I don't even remember their names—probably because I never bothered to learn them. So giving them names that are most likely not the ones they were blessed with isn't out of respect; it's because I simply didn't give a shit about them in the first place. In fact, if they do read this and get offended I couldn't care less. They're the ones with enough egg on their faces to make omelets for an entire Los Angeles basketball team, so fuck them.

That's the kind of book this is going to be: tug on your fucking helmets.

Any-who . . .

I started this night at the hole of holes, the heaven of hells: the Rainbow Bar and Grill. I know—this place appears in so much of my writing that I'd have to cast it as an actual person in any movie made about my life. However, it has always been a giant, beautiful nugget in the gold mine of my absurdities. Thank fuck this story is not a spotlight on *my* dumb shit; I am merely the one who had to witness the buggery. But all tales start somewhere. The starting pistol sounded off at the outside bar, where respectable people can still have a cigarette nuzzled up against finished mahogany while drowning themselves in libations. There's another piece of fine "intelligence": "Hey, I'm going to go inside this place and blow my brains out on alcohol, thereby killing my brain cells and liver while also doing damage to other vital organs. I might even do some blow in the bathroom. But those other fuckers better go outside to SMOKE!" Fuckin' savages . . .

I was hanging out with a friend who had been invited to a party in Silver Lake, a section of LA not too terribly far from the Rainbow. Well, I say not too terribly far: the truth is, I didn't know how far it was—I wasn't driving. All I remember was climbing into my friend's sedan afterward and hanging out the window to let the cool air put the kibosh on my spins. I believe there was even a spirited debate about whether we could cruise through the Del Taco drive-thru for inexpensive meat envelopes. Now that I think about it, I do have a visual of taking a piss behind a dumpster in the parking lot while chatting with a nice gentleman who was none too pleased about the expulsion, maybe because I was singing "And We Danced" by the Hooters at concert volume. People in line at the outside menu couldn't be heard on the speaker. I guess I was calling way too much attention to his rummaging around in those giant canisters for fuck-knows-what. Once I was back in the car and loaded for bear with crappy fast food, we got back on track. Then before I knew it, we were at the party.

In retrospect I can only call it a party in passing. If I can be completely frank, I've had crazier bowel movements. First of all, there were too many dumbasses and not enough chemicals. In other words, there wasn't enough "happy" to go around. Second, the men and women entrenched in this place would make the world's most brain-dead frat brothers look like Mensa members in comparison. It's the same problem I've come across at other parties I've gone to in Hollywood: too much posing and strutting and not enough actual *partying*. You have to remember the kind of people I was used to throwing down with. I was accustomed to maniacs jumping off of roofs and setting walls on fire once they were done sniffing the gasoline fumes. This was basically a bunch of shit heels running around a two-bedroom ranch-style box on a side street in suburban California, trying like hell to look good and catch a buzz before the beer and pills ran out. It didn't exactly move the needle on my RPMs.

I found myself sitting in the middle of a bedroom floor surrounded by atavistic morons, with a redhead on opiates who
was convinced she could read my thoughts and tell me my
future. That would have been simple: the future had me trying
to escape this fucking awful "party." The redhead, who we will
call Janice, was equal parts pretentious, innocuous, and full of
shit. Janice was an actress (an actress in LA . . . what were the
odds?) and was trying out for a role in a health food commercial.
Judging by the shape she was in, I could have told her that she
had an ice cube's chance in Cuba of making that dream a reality. She looked more like Wynonna Judd than Julianne Moore,
complete with the face of a long-haired Clint Eastwood squinting into the desert sun. But being a respectful prick, I kept it
to myself, kindly wished her luck in her endeavors, and made
to take my leave of it all, grabbing for the front doorknob with
one hand and dialing for a cab on my cell phone with the other.
Unfortunately Janice wasn't done with me, much to my chagrin.
I explained to her I was leaving; she asked whether she could
catch a ride back to her apartment. Knowing full well that *nothing* was going to happen with this person, I said sure.

That's when Janice fucked up my night completely.

She said, "Great! Can my friend Charles come along?"

Charles?

It was then that Charles came stumbling up in all of his
embarrassing glory. I had noticed him lurking around the
fringes of the "party" like a sort of B-Movie actor trying too
hard to play a rock-and-roll vampire. Picture Ed Wood meets
Jim Morrison and it all starts to tragically make sense. He was
dressed in black leather pants on a Thursday. Even I know that's
just not cricket—if he were trying to be ironic, I might have cut
him some slack. But I don't think Charles could have spelled
"ironic." To complete this ensemble, he'd matched these pants

up with a sleeveless Ratt T-shirt, a black suit jacket, low-top tennis shoes, and a blue bandana that was more Bret Michaels than Axl Rose. Basically he was shooting for the Izzy Stradlin outfit without being as cool as Izzy Stradlin. Now, I can't say much when it comes to fashion; I myself have a tendency to take good clothes and make bad decisions with them. But even compared to my fashion disasters, this guy looked like a douche pickle soaked in toilet water.

His behavior wasn't helping his Q points at all. He'd been making attempts to engage in conversation with almost everyone, but once he joined a group, he didn't say anything. He just stood there, leaning in a little too close, staring alternately right into your eyes and directly into your chest, leaving the cluster of folks mired with uncomfortable silence and bad breath. When he did say something, all he did was try to pimp his band. But it all came out garbled in vowel sounds and hand gestures. It was as if a rookie mime wanted to hand you a demo tape. At the time I didn't know he was on heroin; I just thought he was wasted—perhaps he'd even resorted to snorting Clorox in the bathroom when all the jubilant goodies were gone. I didn't find out about the heroin until Janice told me later, but we'll get to that. At that moment I just wasn't impressed. Naturally I wasn't very stoked about giving him a ride anywhere. But I was still buzzed enough to be talked into worse shit than that, so I said okay. The cab arrived, I ushered them into the backseat, and I jumped up front. We were all three going separate places, but I assured the cabbie I had ample funds so he would be taken care of.

We'd gone maybe a mile when Charles started to get sick.

I've had my share of satanic moments in the backs of taxis. For all I know, there's a flyer with my face on it tacked onto corkboard in most of the cab stations around the world. But this was distressing. Charles was all over Janice, moaning and clutching at his belly as if we were on the way to the hospital and his water had just broken. There was a lot of thrashing around. Then he kicked the back of my seat. I glanced at the driver, who was now undeniably in the midst of second thoughts about this particular fare. He kept checking his rearview mirror and muttering under his breath about "fuckin' junkies." This was obviously not his first experience with heroin addicts, but it was new for me, and I refused to be subtle about it. I turned around in my seat and stared through the plastic divider that we all know and love in cabs. This was like an episode of *Cop Rock*—so bad you can't take your eyes off of it. It was a novel sensation because normally I was the one who'd screwed the karmic pooch a little too long and was inevitably caught with his dick in the dog. But that wasn't the case this time. I was going to enjoy it . . . or so I thought.

That's when the farting started.

Initially I just laughed like a hyena. Farts make me laugh harder than a whole nation at a Carlin concert. Maybe it's because like most men, my sense of humor stopped developing right around the time I discovered you could make bubbles in the bathwater with a burst of ass air. Whatever the reason, I started fucking HOWLING. Janice didn't appreciate it and laid into me with some passive-aggressive hippie babble: "You know, it's not funny to scoff at another person's pain, Corey. He's coming off of heroin, so his system is really messed up. You might try being a little more empathetic." Fuck all that—this was awesome! I wasn't giggling about the horse DTs; I was giggling at the gas. Not only was I giving a ride to two wastes of dignity, but one was also in the throes of an invisible poop onslaught. Call me a dick all you want—that shit is hilarious. Thankfully we were in California, where you can set your watch to the weather, because the driver cranked all four windows down at once, letting in fresh air to replace the acrid smell invading our territory from the backseat. As much as I was enjoying this Broadway production of a terrible reality show, this shit was starting to get out of hand.

Charles let out a howl that sounded like, "I need to stop and be sick!" I wasn't sure that was a good idea, however; we were deep in the trenches of suburban LA, so really there was nowhere for Charles to do his business. But between Janice's nagging protests and Charles's inaudible pleas, I nudged the driver to pull over on a back street in front of a clutch of one-story duplexes. It was 3 a.m. It was intensely quiet. It was dark as could be. This was the only place I thought was appropriate to take care of this situation. So we slid up to the curb. Janice asked me to go with Charles to make sure he was going to be okay. I didn't want to. I hate people. But I agreed because I knew someday I would need the same type of help from a hapless stranger. Against everything in my fiber, everything in my cellular structure, everything in my mind and everything in my selfish capacity, I made ready to take care of this dildo so I could get back to my own bed as quickly as possible.

We got out of the car.

The following events are *absolutely true*.

I helped Charles creep through the front lawn to a shadowy patch closer to the backyard. I helped him square his stance then backed up quickly—splash back is bad for any man, but splash back from vomit is just cruel and unusual, especially when it's not your own. So I retreated a good distance in order to help if needed but not so close that I would wear his tactical chowder. As if on cue, Charles threw up. Then he threw up and farted simultaneously. I chewed back a gut laugh so the neighbors didn't lynch us. Thinking we were finished here, I stood up a little straighter to help this yutz back to the cab. But apparently Charles wasn't done. With faltering hands and a complete lack of realization for where he was or who was with him, he began to undo his leather pants.

Um, what the fuck, dude?

If you've ever seen someone try to take leather pants off by themselves, you will know how silly it looks. For those of you not privy to this sight, it is in fact futility in motion: it takes two to three pairs of hands, some leverage, and a little traction. Even that requires a little prayer and help from a friend who understands you're not laughing at them, and that's for someone who's *sober*. But this was so far beyond asinine that I thought I was being *Punk'd*. This poor boob of a man was tugging his skintight leathers down in the middle of domestic paradise at an hour when most paperboys are tying their bundles together. I thought to myself, "This prick thinks he's at home. He thinks he's getting ready for bed." Even this was proven to be false, however, when Charles, in a display of mammoth stupidity I had never seen up to that point, stopped pulling his leather pants off at the knees, squatted uncomfortably . . . and began to take a shit. I should qualify that with he was *trying* to take a shit, because it wasn't going well. He fell three times, all of which deposited him into his own pools of sick. When he finally produced turds, the straining and the breaking of winds were almost too much to take. Then the eventual catastrophe happened. After falling in his own puke, Charles finally added masterful insult to monster injury by falling backward onto his own fresh piles of poop. Then, as if it were written in an Edgar Wright screenplay . . . he passed out.

I stood for a second staring at this imbecile, feeling like a burned-out sentinel watching the meteor streak toward the planet, bracing himself for the lethal impact. The Devil's Whisper—the fart that happens just before you run for the bathroom to expel your waste—still hung in the air like the Grim

Reaper blowing you a kiss as he passes by. I was too stunned to speak and too incensed to stutter. But I'm glad I was there, for as I regarded this kiddy pool of a grown child lying in a horrific amalgam of Technicolor Yawn, top soil, and literal shit, certain things started to occur to me: contemplation of my own misdeeds, realization that if I didn't rein in my own uncontrollable urges, I might end up looking as pathetic as this pain in my ass. All of this shot through my big-ass brain in what felt like an eternity but in actuality was possibly just a millisecond. In that moment of clarity a tone was set. I also remembered how early it was in the morning. So I did what anyone with half an IQ would have done in my shabby shoes.

I fucking left him there.

You can boo me all you want. You can talk as many shades of judgmental shit as you like. There was no—*and The Rock means NO*—no fucking way I was letting that fraction of a man, covered in three-fifths of his own fluids (I think he pissed himself when I wasn't looking) get back in the cab with me for any reason. I wasn't going to put that nice taxi driver through it, I wasn't going to put his *cab* through it, and I certainly wasn't going to subject myself to the kind of olfactory assault that would present itself once all of those interesting liquids finished seeping deep into the fabric of his fabulous leather pants. Janice? Hell, I only wish I could have left her there with Captain Dipshit; it was *her* idea to bring him along in the first fucking place. I got in the cab and told the driver to hit the gas. Janice protested, but I quieted her with the knowledge that this was my fare—if she wanted to stay in this car and complain, she could pay for it herself. We dropped her off down the street from her apartment without a good-bye, and I haven't seen her since. On a good day I wish her luck. On a bad day I have hopes that she woke up one morning with her face buried deep in Charles's putrid leather chaos.

It was in that moment long ago, watching a grown man coat himself in excrement and grass stains like a toddler who can't hold its own head up, that I realized something in myself that maybe I had never been asshole enough to see before: when it comes to incompetence and mental oblivion, when it comes to deep-seated stupor and offensive ignorance, my tolerance level is decidedly *low*. Being around stupid, callous people makes me feel like I have the flu: I get aches, I get anxious, I sweat, and I look for any available exit to fight my way to freedom. This is all while trying to restrain myself from lashing out at the offender. My good friend Geoffrey Elizabeth Head once imparted to me a saying that bears repeating: "Son, if you're going to be dumb, be tough because you ain't going to make it on your brains or your looks." Judging by my own observations as of late, this world must be full of tough motherfuckers.

And so we come to the root of this book's evil, bitches.

You see . . . I have been watching you all for a very long time. Yes, as creepy as that sounds, it is unfortunately true. Just as most of you gripping these pages have been following my actions for nearly twenty years, I have been studying your habits and your whims, your qualities and your qualms since before many of you were born. I have observed your shameless daring and your unchecked anger. I have considered your histrionics and your ridiculous gatherings. I have walked among you at event after event, marveling at your behaviors and individualities. Having done so and after all these years, I can unequivocally say that most of you are all so far off the fucking reservation that I fear for the future of our species.

Not the ones who bought this book—you have shown *exceptional* savvy! You are part of the 2 percent that gives me hope! But the other 98 percent of the population, you can simultaneously thank and blame alcohol and YouTube for that statement.

You can also throw some expletives in the directions of reality TV, atrocious drivers, Justin Bieber, Kanye, fast food, infomercials, regular commercials . . . basically just *people*. I've said it before and, Buddha forgive me, I am going to proclaim it again: if it weren't for my family and my friends, I WOULD FuckING HATE YOU ALL, EVERY MOMENT OF EVERY DAY OF MY LIFE.

There are just too many reasons for writing this book, nearly all of which will be headlining the many chapters inside. But I feel it imperative to say this right out of the gate: I am just as guilty of being a meandering cocker as you are. My track record as an occasional mouth-breathing dickhead may have just as many high (low) points as the dozens of "stars" that appear on the assorted TV shows running clip after disturbing clip showing men and women alike making some of the most idiotic moves imaginable. Whether it's selfie footage of women falling through coffee tables while they film themselves twerking or whether it's men shooting each other in the chest with live handguns to show their "toughness" while wearing bulletproof vests, there is an alarming trend of human beings tossing caution to the wind for a trickling glimpse of fame through shame, and what's most sad is they *have* none. They *have* no shame. They don't care that they are spreading moronic activity like a virus across the landscape. They don't give a flying fuck that this shit looks like a live feed from a mental hospital; they just want enough time to throw a bandage on the head wound so they can immediately check to see how many hits the video received in the last twenty seconds. If they took another twenty seconds to watch the video, they might realize they have a concussion.

But I am no Lord of the Hill; these hands pitching fastballs at glass houses are just as dirty as yours are. However, there are a lot of exemptions in my favor. One, much of my calamitous behavior occurred prior to the Digital Age, so no footage or real proof exists (thank fuck) and can only be found in hearsay and interviews. Two, I understand the difference between "getting it out of your system" when you are young and not giving a shit outright about making buffoonery seem like a career and not an aberration as you get old enough to actually know better. Three—and this is most important—it is my book, so I can do no wrong. Shit happens; it just so happens to be yours and not mine. So guess what? Even if you are not devoid of gray matter, even if you are not technically by definition bereft of intuitive mental faculties, you are all guilty by association. This is a RICO case, and I am the district attorney in charge of bringing justice to the world. I may not be infallible, but I can wear a suit and use big words, and it won't even look like someone put peanut butter on the roof of my mouth.

This means I believe most of you can't be trusted to pull the underwear out of your own ass let alone remember to change into clean ones after you have defecated in them. And I hate to say it but you don't make it very difficult to prove my point.

I have a bunch of shit I want to say, and the sad part is there's so much that I don't even know where to start. Airports, megamalls, shitty drivers, family reunions, sex, food, dickless music, clothes, and children—*yes: children*—all of these topics are targets for my venomous brand of vitriol in this book, and it is happening all over the world. As much as most of my international friends and foes would love to believe that this is a singularly American pandemic, I am begging you to give me the chance to differ. I have had the privilege to travel all over this blue, green, and white marble in space. I don't just run around yelling and screaming; I have been known to settle in the background and observe, taking notes when I'm not taking naps on painful, uncomfortable chairs en transit. As much as I realize my country owns its unfair share of stock in this zeitgeist of gibberish, I have also discovered that this is a global catastrophe. I haven't been everywhere, but I've been to enough "wheres" to know that Earth has pockets of stupid popping up north, south, east, and west. From the equator to the prime meridian—dumb does not so easily wash off.

The wonderfully liberating thing about this mounting sense of rage is that I DON'T GIVE A Fuck ANYMORE. I know I've said that in the past, but for better or worse, there has always been a side to me that usually holds a little bit back out of respect and to spare anyone the sting of hurt feelings. Well, as you are about to find out, my gloves are off. Not only are the gloves off, but I've also set fire to them like a Viking Boxer, throwing the burning mitts in a leaky bucket and kicking them across the sea with a hardy sigh and a stout middle finger flown in disrespect. Subsequently, don't get mad at me; you fuckers brought this on yourselves. It's not my fault that your entire population has fallen all over each other to popularize insignificant, irrelevant, talentless garbage. But it'll truly be my sadistic pleasure to rip it all to shreds before your very eyes.

But like I said before, not you guys, readers! We're all cool here. I'm sure none of you would take the Cinnamon Challenge or drink yourselves stupid and pass out with your panties presented for all to see outside the McDonald's in SoHo. I'm unwavering in my assertion that *none* of you would use a ridiculous, pathetic term like YOLO. "You Only Live Once" . . . yeah thanks for that, Confucius. I didn't fucking realize that "You Only Live Once." This is such meaningless, pseudo-analytical bullshit that it makes me madder than anything else at the moment. It'd be one thing if people were using YOLO when it pertained to something meaningful, like climbing a mountain or painting a portrait of that same mountain while sipping exotic teas on a veranda near the sea. I could understand it if you were attempting to put a little culture in your caboose. If YOLO were used in this context, I wouldn't want to shoot spitwads soaked in cunt juice into the face of God. But it's not. It's just fucking not. It's used to excuse the most ignorant, disgusting behavior I have come across in my life, and I grew up in a fucking trailer park in the middle of Nowhere, Iowa. I heard someone use "YOLO" while he tried to convince some idiotic teenage girl to jump sideways onto a moving treadmill while it was going like 60 mph. Guess what: long story short, she ate shit and now her face looks like shit. "You Only Live Once" . . . yeah you only *die* once too, ass hat. A bunch of kids climb into bed to fuck each other crazy—fine, whatever. One says, "You Only Live Once!" Sure, true . . . however, you can get pregnant as many times as your crusty urethras and uteruses can manage. You only live once! You can get herpes and AIDS once as well. Sorry: that shit stays forever. So yes, indeed, you only live once. Let me ask you this: Is it a life worth fucking living?

Oh, but not you exceptional observers of taste and vision! I'm not lumping you into that bacterial pot of oatmeal. No, I have other plans for you. You are going to become my army. You are going to form my Legion of Doom to fight the Regions of Dumb. There's only one requirement for joining this battalion: I need you all to discourage morons from buying this book because this isn't just about stupidity; this is about incompetence. Any person who believes that the shit in this book is okay after I'm done tearing it apart is beyond reproach. This is the difference between a banal mind and an incompetent one. A dumb person can be taught; an incompetent person cannot be taught because he or she has no idea that they are incompetent, thereby making them content to breeze through life knocking people and ideas over in their wakes. So you, my spry little spies, are going

to be the tip of my sword, the gold in my dust. You are all officially Weapons of Mass Disparagement. It is imperative that you
make it absolutely clear to every group of assholes out there that
this book is not for them. Did you take time to read the Foreboding-
ing (Fake) Disclaimer? That shit is real—I had a lawyer look at it.
Okay, so his last name was "Lawyer," but he agreed it felt pretty
binding when I shoved my computer in his face as he delivered
my pizza. So if it looks good to him, it works for me. I indeed
have a wiffle ball bat, and I'm so not afraid to use it. If you have a
bunch of dumb friends and you care for their dumb faces, *do not
let them read this book.*

Make no mistake: this is not the Corey Taylor you see on
the street. This is not the Corey Taylor you run into at meet-
and-greets or in line at the coffee shop. This is not the kind and
cuddly guy that kisses babies and takes pictures with your mom
while leaving a voicemail for that distant cousin in college. This
is not the lovable scamp who can poke just as much fun at himself as he does the various rubes around him. In fact, this isn't
Corey Taylor: this is Corey Motherfucking Taylor. This is The
Great Big Mouth. This is that bastard you wonder about when
you listen to Slipknot. I put the F-U in fuck at any given moment,
and I will fucking sound off with the power of a fistful of mis-
siles. I am going to piss you off while you piss your pants. I am
going to remind you that just as I love to have a good time like
anyone else, I am also a diminutive and angry man with a giant
neck made of muscle, rage, and heavy metal music. I am The
Mouth, and guess what, motherfuckers? The Mouth has had it.
You don't listen. You don't learn. You, unfortunately, don't like
to do anything other than chase the shiny baboon ass of fame,
fortune, and frivolous attention grabbers. You treat each other
so shabbily that I can't do anything but sit on my couch and
seethe like a criminal. I can't go out in public because you all act

like fuck licks. I can't go on the Internet because now that everyone has a voice, no one is saying anything that is worth hearing or reading. I can't watch TV because it is so overloaded with reminders that the Earth is fucked that I hide under my bed in case a dickhead with a machete comes charging into my house. Great—you're all dumb *and* nuts. I guess it's time to turn The Vault into a Panic Room. At least I won't be bored: that's where all my DVDs and comic books are kept. It would only make sense to install an entertainment center, complete with monitors so I can watch the outside of my house. You never know when someone's going to snap and turn into Jason Voorhees.

I'm going to wrap this chapter up so we can get to the beating hearts of the matters that just don't matter, and I am going to do so by describing to you the last bit of weirdness I was a part of not too long ago.

We had a party at Chez Taylor for my son Griffin's birthday. There was a part of me that was weeping because my little man was growing up. There was also a part of me that was proud to see how he was growing up. So I let him decide on the theme for the party and I went to work on getting it all together. I decided to buy him a cake instead of baking one as I have done for the last seven years. This afforded me a glimpse into my own boobery because the cake I got was *way* too big: one full cookie sheet and two stories high, covered in mouth-watering cream cheese frosting. Side note: we were *still* eating off this monster a week later. I finally had to throw it away, and it was *still* big enough for another birthday party.

I'm an idiot . . .

This isn't about the cake, though. This is about one of Griffin's friends. We made some invites for Griff to take to school so his friends could come over. Within an hour the house was crawling with kids Griffin's age, hopped up on sugar and running around like suicide bombers on a day off. Let me tell you something really quick: I love my children. I do. However, I am really not fond of other people's children, including some of my closest friends' kids. Really, I just hate them. I'm a decent enough guy not to say it to their faces, but it's true. To me, most kids are fucking mobile diseases with opposable thumbs and vocal cords. But I can usually keep it to myself. There is, however, one of Griff's friends who strains my patience against the Kevlar skin I use to keep it in check. Now, I'm a not complete cunt—I won't tell his real name. Not that I'm worried about this kid reading any of my books; Griff and his friends roll their eyes for the most part at my so-called fame. But I won't tell you his name because, on the off chance that it gets back to him, he's weird enough to try to come at me with a butter knife or some garden shears—whatever might be in reach. So for the sake of my safety, we'll call him Milt.

At the birthday party he calmly informed me that I was taking him home . . . without asking me beforehand. I let a little anger slip when I replied that next time he needed to ask me first because, and I quote, "I don't really want to!" However, I spoke with his mother and assured her that I would in fact bring Milt home after the party had come to a close. Milt was very happy—he didn't want to leave his friends behind too soon. Around 8:30 p.m. the other parents had swung by and dragged their kids off to their respective homes. I escorted Milt to the family Range Rover, and we began the short drive to his house.

Now, I know this kid was young, but I can usually hold a conversation with anyone of any age. This would not be the case on this ride into central Des Moines. Oh I tried. I tossed out one-liners in various attempts to have a nice talk with Milt. But all I got was one-word replies.

"So how's school treating you?"

"Good."

Silence.

"You'll have to give me a head's up when we get close to your house—I'm not sure exactly how to get there, okay?"

"Yeah."

Silence.

"Have a good time at the party?"

"Yep."

Silence.

It was after that last one that a sound began catching my ear from the backseat. At first I couldn't quite place it: it sounded like someone was simultaneously sucking the spit from their mouth and snorting the snot from their nose back into their head.

SSSHHCREEEEENT.

What the? . . .

I tossed a glance in the rearview mirror and looked at Milt. He was sitting quietly, staring out the window and watching the scenery fly by on the freeway. He looked tranquil; I didn't think a sound that violent could have come from him. I returned my gaze back to the road and was just turning the radio up so I could focus on some music instead of the dead air when it happened again, but this time even louder.

SSSHHCREEEEENT!

I looked back at Milt again: not a damn sausage. It *had* to be him making the noise. I figured he had a stuffy nose so I asked him if he would like a tissue.

"Nope."

Silence.

Then . . .

SSSHHCREEEEENT!

I was so preoccupied with trying to catch him making the noise that I missed the turn to get him to his house. He was supposed to remind before I got there, not *after*—which he did . . . and then made that noise again. This time I saw it! He wasn't snotty, full of phlegm, or anything; he was just making the noise with his mouth as he stared out the window. What the fuck is *with* this kid?

I got him to his house and pulled into his driveway. Without saying another word, he jumped out of the backseat, slammed my goddamn door, and sauntered slowly up to his house, where his father was waiting for him on the steps. I sat there trying to understand what had just happened, and as I did I heard him make that noise one last time as he went in his house.

SSSHHCREEEEENT!

At least he'd waved good-bye as he did it.

Nothing against Milt, but he's a crazy little shithead. He is also one of the reasons I am writing this fucking book. Those fucking popcorn shrimp . . . sorry, that's giving too much away. You'll understand when we talk more about him later on.

You see, I can handle adults wallowing in their individual dumbass quagmires. You're all for the most part mature and old enough to do whatever you want with your lives. If you want to be ignorant wretches, that's your right; all I can do is add something new and better to the menu above the Slurpee counter. But our kids are another matter. They are growing up bombarded with images and words worthy of profound ridicule. Worse yet, they are being taught that *this shit is okay*. But it is *not* okay. For fuck's sake, *it is not okay*. It's a travesty to our nature and propensity to evolve. The fact that children are growing up having to push through a foundation of shit just to find their place in this world is unfair. We should be discouraging their exposure to the worst bits or at the very least explaining to them that this is aberrant behavior and they shouldn't engage in it. That's what we do with our kids in the Bonnici/Bennett/Taylor family hybrid.

That's what I feel we all must do around the world before the next generation grows up in perpetual need of having their adult diapers changed while they post pics on PoopTube for their friends to make crappy comments (pun intended) about their latest shit mosaic. That's not a Rorschach Test—that's a mess.

So strap yourselves to the seats, fuckers. As I have always said when I start these feeble clothbound attempts at reason, you don't have to agree with me. But that doesn't mean I am wrong. I may be an asshole, but I'm not wrong. Just because the world can read it doesn't mean they understand what's being inferred. I've been studying you for a long time, as I've said. I know what you're capable of just as much as I know what you've been up to. No offense, Earth, but . . .

Sigh.

I'm going to pretend that you are all fucking dumb.

Proceed with caution.

CHAPTER 2

FUCKED IN PUBLIC

Before I commence to hacking my way through the treacherous wilds and heady navigations that forced me to write this vile diatribe in the first place, let's get to know the "star" of this Broadway production: humans. You're right, of course: considering that I'm terrified by a myriad assortment of species like sharks, spiders, and tree sloths, you'd think I'd have a bigger beef with the rest of the dinner party taking place outside our end of the animal kingdom. Sadly, this is not the case. "Haters gonna hate," or so my iPod has led me to believe. So let's get to the soft meaty gooch of this chapter's query.

Have you people fucking paid attention to each other lately?

Seriously? By that I don't mean the Delphic maxim "Know thyself" jibber jabber; I mean have you really taken a look at yourself with some clarity (no eye boogers) and noticed how ridiculous you are all behaving? Huh? I have to be honest: I don't think you are. If you were, you'd have realized long ago that the roaming packs of raging morons that most of you tend to comprise when you go "out on the town" are making us *all* look like shit. From Vegas to South Beach, from Cabo San Lucas to the French Quarter, all over America and beyond, the masses are frothing and scrambling from bar to bar, street to street, hovel to hovel, searching in earnest for the next buzz, the next free one. They all make it seem like real life is so bad that they can't handle being sober to enjoy it, which is utter fucking drivel. But if eyewitness accounts are to be allowed into evidence, they don't need alcohol to act the fool.

Let's start with this global "party scene." Trust me: I see it all over the world. Most of the belligerence starts at night, and yet the seeds for this universal embarrassment are planted while the sun still blazes high above us. Apparently you don't even have to have a *job* these days to be so stressed and tested you need to go out and blow your mind on bootleg gingers and high shines. I could understand this shit more if it were just nine-to-fivers embalming themselves. Even college kids could get a pass— that's a lot of pressure for a mind that hasn't sufficiently finished developing. But from my standpoint many of those who butcher the conventions of public decency are young, lazy layabouts. They do fuck all in the a.m. but sleep. The p.m. is reserved for finding out what they'll be up to while they're missing late-night television. I know what I'm talking about: I used to be one of those people . . . when I was nineteen. Being young was kind of a requirement for this oafish bollocks. Nowadays, well, let's just say it wouldn't be a shock to come across a coven of bastards and bitches, all of differing ages, trying desperately to do beer bong hits together on a Wednesday night whilst hanging out of a third-story balcony at a Best Western hotel. I suppose if you're going to set an example, you better be able to walk the walk. About an hour later, however, they're all out on the streets, *wasted.* That's just what we need right now. Oh, wait—actually no, it's in fact the exact opposite.

If you don't spend as much time as I do strolling the streets of various metropolitan byways inadvertently engaged in anthropological research, just switch on your TV sets—if you can stomach it. Every network on the dial or dish has a variety of programs all showing the glamour and glut of so-called reality shows, the worst idea in the history of programming since Geraldo went digging for Al Capone's recyclables. All of these shows have several things in common: the "cast" are dicks, they spend all day bitching at or about each other, and at night they just *have* to blow off some steam, what with all the energy they spent doing *nothing* all day, unless you count the aforementioned high-speed bitch attacks. So these same cunt-face people load up on chemicals and cocktails, only to have the inevitable clash of hairy cat shit right before the producers cut to commercial. It's a gross mess devoid of class, morality, or even a working vocabulary because half the time they're speaking in beeps. I didn't know high-pitched squeals were in the English language. Well, it's either that or these fuckwads use so many curse words it's amazing they got on the telly in the first place. But people around the world are mesmerized by this trash, and by calling it "reality TV," they believe this is how everyone lives, so they decide to do so in turn. Can I get a "hell yeah" for the human race? Before you go hip-hip-hooraying, though, remember that this shit makes me want to stab squirrels in their cute little innocent faces with a ballpoint pen.

It's no wonder we're all a mess in public, then. All we see and hear is crap, so we have to be crappy to blend in. That's the cattle mentality: it's always easier to follow the herd than it is to go find better cud somewhere else on your own. The blame also goes to the producers of this calamitous form of entertainment. They make sure that all the hands involved on the screen are going to be venomous harpies, then they throw a bunch of "story arcs" their way in hopes that it will stir up the kind of controversy the networks are looking for. It is a maddeningly rich racket that they are milking at every nipple. Shore to shore, Jersey or Geordie, the cameras are getting close-ups on all the festering boils that the gene pool has to offer, and the entranced huddled masses are following suit. This is one of the reasons why I believe public intoxication, drunk driving, arrest rates, and subsequent related deaths are at a twenty-year high all over the planet. What really makes me angry on a nuclear level is that no one is doing anything about it.

But let's get back to my original posit: Are any of you privy to how dumb you all look? First of all, you all dress the same. The guys all look like they bought the same shitty button-up shirts at the same strip mall, along with the brand-name pants with shiny shit on the ass. Good call, guys: you look like rapists. The sad thing is you probably are, convicted or not. You are one roofie away from your own personal pink card and having to legally live a certain distance away from schools and nurseries. We shouldn't forget the hair gel and the *constant* sweating. If nervous porcupines could stand and walk upright, they would all look like the men of the world. Between the race to see how many shots you can do in sixty minutes and the high fives, chest bumps, and screaming in each other's faces like you just scored a touchdown, I'm amazed we've been able to propagate humanity at all. It's a fucking wonder women consider having sex with any of us. Oh, that's right—women are just as bad.

Ninety-eight percent of you girls wear shoes you can't walk in, clothes that don't fit, and dresses or skirts that don't cover your bulbous asses. You scream and giggle at each other like you're in third grade while casting a wary eye about for "bitches" that might encroach on your territory. When you feel sufficiently safe, you stand in a circle and do shots off of each other's tits. Then you complain when the men in the vicinity start treating you like hookers, even as you're being dragged to the bathroom for a quick blowjob. All of this culminates in a sad, drunken walk to a car or a cab, whether you're going home or to some guy's house, ending with you falling over in your stupid shoes, dress hiked up, ill-fitting panties hanging out, and a depressing video on YouTube in which you try in pure inebriation to get back up, looking like a turtle in drag that unfortunately ended up on its shell. I watch all those videos, and they are all fucking hilarious. Then I find myself wanting to slit my wrists because of how painfully sad they all are. Is this where we are? Is this what we're left with? We're all coming off as pretty petty and pathetic, and the brutal facts point out that the evidence supports this theory wholeheartedly.

It doesn't really help our cause that there are giant constructs designed to lure the platypuses to the fuckfest. Sodom and Gomorrah had nothing on the cities drawing the diseased to their bosoms: Vegas, LA, South Padre, South Beach, New Orleans, Austin . . . America may not have the patent on the urban need to pub crawl, but they have definitely upped the ante in a lot of ways. It's the red, white, and blue way: take something that may have been designed for joy and pleasure, inject it with steroids and bacon grease, throw a grenade in it, and build a giant adult theme park as a beacon for the soiled, charging way too much as they make us pay with something other than money. Sometimes it just really sucks to be American, especially when I know just how much potential this country has for greatness and acceptance. But I don't dwell; I just make voodoo dolls. Someday soon those things are going to work.

As always, I digress . . .

If only the facsimile of ridicule was just relegated to the nightlife, I wouldn't be going off on this particular tangent. Oh no: this self-important opera plays itself out at all hours. You see it everywhere. I could do a dissertation on coffee shops *alone*. You know that feeling? I walked into a Starbucks the other day and, as usual—with my sunglasses on so people didn't notice me staring—I studied the various customers around me from my vantage point in line. Starbucks never lets me down. Free Wi-Fi and caffeine bring out the inner dipshit just as strongly as Jack Daniels and Grey Goose. Tables are filled to bursting with writers, pumping out script after script that most likely will never be committed to film. If they're not punching up scenes, they are working on their manuscripts in hopes that a publishing house *really* has a division dedicated to fan fiction involving *Harry Potter*, Superman, and a multisexual duck with several sets of genitalia. As flattered as I was to receive that particular story, I would be remiss if I didn't say I was uncomfortable passing it on to people who trust my judgment.

One day, while waiting to order my usual mix of java and Yeah Dawg, there was a woman jogging in place, fresh from her morning run—or at least that's what she wanted us to think—talking rather loudly into her headset Bluetooth device at a colleague she obviously had seniority over. The conversation was long-winded, innocuous, and holding up the line: she was actually doing this at the counter while ignoring the "coffee barista" who was trying to take her order. The lady wasn't even looking at him; she was just barking into her NSYNC microphone: "No, *no*, NO! You can't *do* that! There's obviously been a misunderstanding on *their* part!" I couldn't take it anymore and leaned behind her, essentially cutting her in line. Now I deplore queue barging as much as the next dude, but I was in a hurry and didn't want to stand there waiting for the Queen of Douche to place her order, which was most likely going to be some sort of soy-smoothie-berry-green tea concoction that, in my eyes, honestly has no place in a coffee shop. As I did so, she suddenly came to life. "Hey—hold on a second, Martha. Hey! I was next in line!"

I calmly looked her in the face and said, "Get off your phone then and make your order."

She replied with, "You can't talk to me like that!"

To which I responded with, "If you're on your phone, then you're not in line. Sorry."

And the barista agreed with me. Her Majesty the Bitch left in a huff, jogging all the way.

That is just one example of a Taylor Trigger: self-righteous indignation. When people suffer under the illusion that their time and attention is more important than everyone else's, no matter how mundane the occasion may be, I snap like a piece of dried-up driftwood, waiting to be set fire at the pyre. Some might think that, given my station in the world and what I do for a living, I would have those very same impulses to imply that my fecal contributions have no malodorous air. Guess what, fuckers? My shit does indeed stink, and even though I might have been an insufferable cunt at times in my youth, I make a concentrated effort to avoid that sort of behavior at all costs. I may be an asshole, but I am no ball bag.

At least I hope not anyway.

Getting back to the bull pucky, idiocy is tragically not relegated to the anal annals of the worldwide coffee shops. The malls of America certainly conjure up some serious reasoning for government-enforced sterilization. The funny thing is that presently there are three different *kinds* of mall in the world.

When I was growing up, there was just the local mall: each side of town had its own, and they were pretty much just a representation of the people who lived there. So basically malls were a great way to get a feel for what that side of town had to offer— the poor side, the blue-collar side, the rich side, and so forth. However, businesses evolve right alongside the animals and plants that are the denizens of Earth, 90210. The mall as I knew it began to shift and change. People started flocking to them for different reasons, in turn causing the malls themselves to cater to certain beings and a specific type of commerce. Thus began the new age of the mall and its three different specificities.

First, there is the Dirt Mall. It was once the poor mall, but as the need for money outweighed the needs of the few, the major outlets slowly moved away from this once fairly interesting place. As the big chains moved out, however, the "locals" moved in. This gave rise to what you would consider the "trinket trade." I'll give you an idea of what I mean. The mall I used to go to when I was a kid was a hop, skip, and a jumped ignition from my Gram's house on the South Side of Des Moines, Iowa. It used to be a cobbled combo of the usual suspects: JC Penney, Sears, Target, and a bunch of other norms in between, like Claire's Boutique, a record store called Disc Jockey (where I once worked), Spencer's Gifts, Game Shop for video games, and so on. It was a regular mall with regular people—it was great fun. I was once nearly arrested for going there with no shoes on because apparently "attempted use of alleged Athlete's Foot" is considered a misdemeanor in Des Moines. But I never held that debacle against the place, nor was I angry at the mall when I was fired from the record store for having long hair. I was cool; things were fine.

Anyway, years later we got signed; I went out on tour and didn't go to that mall for a long time. When I did step foot back inside,

I was fairly put off by what I saw. Gone were the chain stores and other shop fronts. In their places were stores that offered Chinese throwing stars, jade statuettes, and whole professional kits for crochet. There were shops offering New Age "medical" attention, encouraging the customers to invest in "the healing power of pretty-colored stones and herbs." Some of the spaces weren't even occupied; they were just empty, giving the mall the feeling of being inside a mouth that was losing teeth at an alarming rate. The most high-profile places were the Animal Rescue League and a bank. There were *three* separate play areas for children, all of which had the same vibe a traveling carnival gives off when it's the last day and the carneys desperately just want to pack up and go home. Nothing about the mall was inviting; it was like a ghost town after the gold was gone. This was the birth of the Dirt Mall in Des Moines.

As I said, though, there are three kinds of mall now, and my town has an example of them all. The Dirt Mall is on the south side. But there are two malls in town that fall under the second category: the No-Other-Alternative-Here Mall. This is the mall you go to when you can't find what you're looking for anywhere else. You don't really want to, but fuck, what are you supposed to do? You *have* to have that sweater vest! It's not even a choice at that point—it's a fucking challenge. And if going to the No-Other-Alternative-Here Mall—or NOAH Mall—means you get that sweater vest, then by god and clean jeans, you are *going* to the NOAH Mall . . . and hell's coming with you.

There are, in fact, two NOAH Malls in my hometown, and both started out on very different ends of the spectrum. One was in fact another blue-collar mall at one time and had gone through multiple fluctuations fiscally in its years of wear and tear; sometimes it would trend poor, and other times it would flex toward flush. It had steady business, however, and held as much ground as it seemed to give. The other mall had at one time, ironically, been the rich mall. It was located on the west side and the lifeblood that ran through its veins over the years had been the wealthy of our little side of the Midwest. It was upper class, snobby, and *reeked* of Drakar cologne. Over the decades these two monoliths of money had duked it out even though each one knew who was winning the fight on any given Sunday. As they did, more land was being developed farther west, spreading the gift of suburban high jinks to the exits off the highway folks rarely traveled. Pretty soon the blank spaces of west Des Moines were colored in with families and fun.

That is when the *real* Rich Mall moved in.

Two stories high and damn near the biggest thing the city had ever experienced, Jordan Creek had quickly put to rest the argument of where the wealthy people in town were going for their socks and signets. The other two malls really never stood a chance. At Jordan Creek, on any day of the week, you can buy— and this is true—swords, guns, pretzels, $500 tennis shoes, Yankee Candles, DVDs, lingerie, whatever the hell Bath & Body Works sells, books, coffee, and Love Sacks, which are plush bean bag chairs the size of a Honda Accord. There are more restaurants at that mall than on the south side alone and a theater that might as well be on Hollywood Boulevard. Oh, and they have a Cheesecake Factory.

Game. Set. Match.

For the poor fuckers at the NOAH Malls, all they could do was pour a little more money into décor and ambience just to keep enough of their heads above water so they weren't choking on salt and saliva. Jordan Creek was *carpeted*, with fountains and elevators, for Christ's sake. If Zeus himself was going to shop at the Gap, he was going to go to Jordan Creek. With

Jordan Creek's construction, the mall battles of Des Moines, Iowa, were swiftly drawn to a bloody close, shortening the war by four years. But by doing so, Jordan Creek had in fact evoked the universal sin of all sins. It had given rise to the worst of the worst: the *real* mall shoppers. People were now bopping along, paying no attention, cracking off into their cell phones and cackling at unheard shitty jokes like they were front row for the second coming of Pryor. Keys dangling from manicured fists, these sophomoric twits blazed a terrible trail through our midst with enough selfish ambiguity to place us all on the chopping block, with no turning back. These are grim times in the DSM, and there seems to be no resistance to its allure. Teenagers, both girls and boys, rummage through the psyches of the platitudes, skulking or pointing, acting like assholes on parole. We'll talk *way* more about children later, but suffice it to say that the landscape is riddled with shit stains with too much time on their hands. And many of them aren't buying a fucking thing.

Never mind the mall walkers . . . here's the Sex Pistols.

I have put up with shit like flash mobs and Occupy Restrooms for so long you're all lucky I haven't climbed a fucking clock tower in recent years. In fact, why are so many of you out and about during the day? I know for a fact that most of you don't have the kind of freewheeling schedule that I enjoy. Where are your jobs? What do you *do* for a living? And if you don't have a fucking job, why the hell are you buying so much shit you really don't need? Are your parents away on vacation? Did you bolt on your sitters? Did you sneak out the window of your bedroom in broad daylight like a "cast" member on *Cops* so you could peruse the streets and cul-de-sacs of the world for no real reason? I suppose I could be considered a callous cock face for this, but my question is: What do you actually *do*?

According to the commercials of the world, set annoyingly to that shitty Indy hippie garbage (we'll talk more about that "music" later), what you people do with your time is simple: you traipse through sunlit afternoons, creating unique activities for yourselves because your generation is *so* different, you have to have different things to engage your independent and, therefore, superior attention. You have impromptu kickball games or paint things that you consider ugly and displeasing to your eyes. You gather in public places to make art consisting of multicolored cardboard cutouts that you then hold up to the sky in certain shapes while someone with a modified iPhone pretends to be Helmut fucking Newton on a roof somewhere, shooting from above in a subliminal nod to how you consider yourself looking down on the crowd because you "know it's more dramatic." You all dress differently and, by doing so, dress exactly the same, with your clever T-shirts of icons you have no clue about, pants that are so tight, they should technically be cutting off the blood flow to your ankles, and black horn-rimmed glasses, whether you need them or not, all tied nicely together with a seemingly inexpensive-yet-very-expensive corduroy jacket. You love fun and life and happiness and bullshit because you are all unequivocally *the* most pretentious bunch of cocksuckers I have ever seen. At least the Yuppies owned their shit. You treat everything you do as vital because if you don't, you'd be faced with the reality that you have no fucking clue what you're doing or what you're supposed to do next.

I know what you're thinking. You're saying to yourself, "What do you mean, 'you people'?" To which I will retort, "What do *you* mean, 'you people'?" I warned you before: this wasn't going to go well for you, so suck your straws until the cup is dry and shut up. Everywhere I look there are scores of cunts just moseying through their tenure with not a care in the world. Meanwhile, people are homeless. Children are dying. Animals are mistreated. Families are torn asunder. Countries collide above our heads, and our government officials can't even stand being in the same room with each other. Yeah, these are all great reasons to muck about and suck at life. Your "can-do" attitudes only really get as far as what you *feel* like doing for *yourselves*.

Some of you hippie types might actually be bothered to join the fight here and there where the chains show a bit of abuse, but when you do it's always done so fucking twat-like. I saw a commercial on a relatively new network in the states where a correspondent was attending an "alternative music festival." The shit they had at this festival was such twaddle that I couldn't stand myself. A woman was selling poetry at a typewriter. A man was making albums at a vinyl press. An "artist" was creating "art" on an LED screen and having people stand in front of it while he took their pictures—trouble is, it was the same pair of crappy angel wings every time. But to the washed masses, this was the epicenter of art in this country. I've seen more thought-provoking roadkill. These same people were bragging about recycling. Yay fucking Bertha: you're *supposed* to fucking recycle. What do you want, a cookie soaked in Nobel Prizes? Go fuck yourself, you self-important dildos. Having said that, it occurs to me that that may in fact be the only way they can experience satisfaction: by fucking themselves. So the joke's on me.

And I'm not fucking laughing.

You could set your watch to how incredibly benign people and their ilk behave in this day and at their age. The problem is that I know this type of youthful renaissance fascinates the rest of my kind. My fellow water buffalo stop in their muddy tracks, taken in by the strange goings-on of this aberrant movement.

At this moment in history distraction is the name of the game. Don't pay any mind to the seriousness of our places in the world. Don't worry whether Egypt is burning, Libya is crumbling, and South America is still anathema for anyone *not* in a drug cartel. Don't you worry your pretty little fuck faces about a goddamn thing. Just make sure those mittens you knit for yourself match the embroidered jumper you got for Christmas. Be lucky I'm not God: I would have canceled this shit-ass experiment called Man long before Jimmy Fallon got his own talk show.

I need to get outside my sweatbox and clear my head for a bit. So I'll tell you a story that, though it gets heavy at the end, is about the joy of being yourself and the hell that is other people, to paraphrase Sartre. You see, being a geek at heart, there are certain places I have longed to make pilgrimages to since before I could sing in tongues. I have always wanted to go on a Civil War tour and visit the essential hot spots tied to that ordeal. I want to take my wife to Egypt so we can stand in front of the pyramids and gaze in wide-eyed wonder (also because I want to get to the bottom of what *Ancient Aliens* is going on about). At some point in my career I want to play the Hollywood Bowl—as much for the prestige as for the fact that my heroes, from Jim Morrison to Monty Python, have all played that beautiful place near the 101. I have places I want to go and experiences I want to cherish. So you can imagine my furious excitement when I was asked to be a part of a special signing at the San Diego Comic-Con, the Mecca for ink rats like me.

I was so elated that I packed all my good comic book T-shirts, but I was also pragmatic enough to make sure there was ample room in my suitcase for all the things I was going to buy while I wandered the cavernous bowels of the happiest place on Earth for comic nerds. I had a plan, and I wasn't going to let anyone sway me from my objective: to get my grubby little hands on all the stuff I'd ever wanted to own as a child. I believe this is the stuff of legend for collectors, although it could also be considered the starting gun for a hoarder-to-be. But I didn't care. I was going in wallets blazing and holidays be damned. The cool thing was I could bring my family, including Griff, my nieces Haven and Jaylynn, and my nephews Drew and Lil Phil. My wife, sister, and mother-in-law followed suit, if only to watch the Grown Man-Boy go ape shit at the sight of so many action figures and so little time. Shit was real; punch that shit.

I did my signing at the Dark Horse booth in the middle of the convention center and had a great time hanging out with fans and artists alike. I was giddy—the place was wall-to-wall Kick Asteroid, and I was in love with every minute of it. Everywhere I looked there was a wall covered in stuff I had to have to survive: a *Doctor Who* bathrobe that looked like the Tardis (I bought it), *Dexter* fan art (I bought it), Lego sets I had never seen before (of course I bought a few), and a whole slew of Minecraft toys for the kids. Oh by the way, I bought them. I was daunted at first when I couldn't find many of the back-issue comics I was looking for, but that paled in the face of the fact that I was with my family in a giant room surrounded with anything else my heart could long for. However, the venom was about to present itself inside the pretty flower.

After making the rounds and checking it all out, we decided to find a restaurant somewhere and grab some foodstuffs. A couple of hours later we were making our way back to the hotel near the Con. It was during this journey back to our rented digs that we ran face-to-ass into a blockade that any man, woman, or child would shudder to find themselves immersed in. The sun had gone down. The nightlife had come to those sad streets.

And much to my chagrin and the extreme discomfort of my family, the sidewalks and roads were bloated with the preposterous pageantry I like to call "douche soup."

Everywhere we looked, dick holes stuffed into Affliction clothing were spilling out into the street, drunk and dumb. Everywhere I turned, party chicks were flashing badger with balloons shaped like cocks for misguided headgear. As we drove we became boxed in by two very different types of transport. One was a limo covered in very suggestive writing and containing what appeared to be a lascivious bachelorette party hanging out of every orifice the vehicle had and screaming bloody murder, spilling drinks and body parts in their wake. The other was a very, *very* expensive Aston Martin DB9 cruising the concrete like a king on sabbatical. The tool shed behind the wheel looked greasy, slimy, and a little too tanned. Plus, with that badass car at his disposal, he was driving WAY TOO FuckING SLOW. I understood immediately: What was the point of having a car like that if no one could see you driving it? So Captain Butt Munch was basically in neutral, winding through the San Diego byways doing a maximum speed of half a mile per hour. It was infuriating. Between the professional alcoholics exploding from the local bars and the dinguses polluting traffic, I felt like I was stuck in gridlock at a Mardi Gras parade. This place I had waited so long to visit had become everything I had learned to hate: pretentious, overindulgent, and disgusting. Needless to say, it knocked the sparkle off of my Apple Jacks.

Then it went from bad to worse.

We found out the hard way that, the way the streets are set up in that part of San Diego, there was only one road that went across the tracks, around the convention center, and to our hotel. Unfortunately for us, we got lost twice trying to find that one sliver of cement bound for freedom. This meant we had to drive through the melee another two times before we could get back and go to sleep. It seemed like every time we made our way through the chaos, we saw something even more offensive than before. I've witnessed some serious shit in my life—I've been to Holland, for fuck's sake—and even I was flabbergasted, to use that word for forty points. If I hated people before, I was on the verge of homicide after that night. I don't think I'll ever go back, and if I do, I certainly won't take my children. When life gives you douche soup, send it back to the chef, because it's clearly not what you ordered to begin with.

It could be karma.

Look, I'm not an idiot. I know I have "sinned" as much as anyone else dragging knuckles around here. We'll get to my "transgressions" eventually, and I promise I won't hold anything back. But, man, I got to be honest: you're making me hate you. That shit sucks, because I don't *want* to hate you. I love you fucking shit brains. Every day I'm reminded of all the great things I love so much about the human race: good people fighting the ignorance and hate all over America; Muslim women standing stronger and taller in the face of intolerance by most of the males of Islam; Russians coming closer and closer to battling the antiquated mindsets that deal with homosexuality in their country; sciences and religions moving forward together to find the divine middle so they can better understand each other. I could write albums' worth of lyrics full of the things that endear me to the beasts I call my fellow humans. And yet here I am, ripping shit to shreds because the louder noises are all incoherent blasts of incompetent screaming. When I'm talking to someone I can really tell has absolutely no clue about what they are babbling about, all I hear is Mr. Krueger's sharp metal nails being dragged across a chalkboard seemingly without end. I can't remember who said it, but there's a great saying that goes,

"Dumb should hurt." I couldn't agree more, because other people's dumb shit hurts me all the fucking time.

I'm a firm believer in balance. In life and all its trimmings there should exist a fifty-fifty pendulum that is perpetually swinging in everyone's favor. The Haves should share the burdens of the Have-Nots and vice versa. But at this moment in this place on this dimensional plain, that shift is flying more out of sync than a drunken boy band trying out for Simon Cowell on his swag yacht. I could sit back and ignore it, like most of the fair intelligentsia around the world. However, I don't work that way. When something's fucked, I blurt it out, whether anyone's listening or not. When the going gets stupid, I can't just get out of the way. I will crash down with a spiteful hammer, like Thor with a death wish, reaping the whirlwind and using big words so no one around me knows what the hell I'm talking about. Simply put, I just don't give a shit anymore. No one has any common sense. No one has any sense of morality. No one has any clue what they should be doing. If this were a factory floor, the place would be empty and littered with body parts because everyone would be at home nursing an injury and drawing workman's comp. I'm trying to not let it get me down, but more and more every day I can't get the music loud enough to drown you all out. I'll go deaf before I go numb, though. So fucking be it.

In closing this chapter let me just gently point you in the right direction: pay attention when you're out and about in this world we all share. Be aware of what's going on and savvy about your actions. Start with something simple like . . . oh I don't know . . . hurry the fuck up when you're crossing the street. I mean that. You all just sort of saunter from corner to corner like you don't know where you are. It's not funny anymore. All you have to do is jog five feet, and you're halfway there already. This is more of a coast-to-coast problem, as in California where people are too busy posing and in New York where people just ignore you. But it's spreading all over the world at an alarming rate. You wander out into oncoming traffic with your stupid faces buried in your cell phones, texting or talking or otherwise, acting like what you're doing is far more important than the rest of the millions of lives being held up by your inactivity. Stop texting—the person you're communicating with isn't going to laugh at your joke or the smiley fucking face you send them. Stop talking—your conversation is not that essential to anyone's life, including your own. Cross the goddamn street so we can all take care of our own bullshit.

I don't care if you're walking your dogs. I don't care if you're walking your kids. I don't care how old or young you are. I don't care if you have one or more legs. Move your fucking ass. This light isn't going to stay green forever, and I need to make a right fucking turn. Never mind why I'm in such a hellfire rush to get to where I'm going; I have my own idiocy to take care of, and I need to do it right now! If you don't get the lead out of your legs, I won't hit you with my car. We're way past that. What I *will* do is shit directly into my hand and throw it like a fastball into your hair. You're turning me into a chimpanzee in a drive-by. So start with that. Then we'll move on from there.

The tomfoolery of the outdoors has brought me to the point of violent alacrity. Vesuvius has nothing on this Irish prick here. I will ride a monstrous war cow into your numbers, flailing a mighty mace of punishment without a care for who it takes to the ground. You're all guilty, so you're all getting the brunt of my bombast. None of you are impressive. None of you are special. None of you are exempt. I know that spits in the face of everything we learned in Sunday school and kindergarten, but it's true, and painfully so. Nobody gives a shit anymore, and it shows. Nobody takes the time to see what his or her actions are doing, and it's all over the page like a rash of punctuation that doesn't belong there.

That's a bit too heavy. Let me put it another way.

There is a hard-wired craving inside us all to fit in and be liked, no matter how cantankerous or embittered we have all become. It's a primal instinct to band together in tribes or groups for safety, to know we are going to be okay. I'm no different; you're no different—it's like never wanting to be picked last for kickball. Things like this are vital to how we feel about ourselves and how we make our way through the world. So that makes us susceptible to even the most ridiculous sorts of behaviors, especially in public. Everyone else is behaving like shit, so why shouldn't I, right? Hell, I can relate. I once spent two horrid weeks talking like Pauly Shore because all of my friends in high school were doing the same. But I came to with a shocked start and made damn sure I never did it again. Cool, buuuuuuddy! May-Jor! Sorry—sometimes it's so much fun I just can't resist falling back into bad habits. Anyway, from my own experience I know the pressure to be a part of the giant mixer of life. But the things I'm seeing you do out in the open are inexcusable. I would go so far as to say you're making us all look bad, but unfortunately everyone is doing it. All I can say truthfully is that you're making a small percentage of us look bad. That probably doesn't pass much mustard for the majority of the abhorred, but with me it's a bit of a source of rancor that I can't let slide anymore.

But no one's listening right now, no matter how loud I scream. All I can do is wait . . . wait for you all to come to your dulled senses and feel the warmth of embarrassment spread through your rosy cheeks. Mind you, I don't know how long I can tolerate the tension as I wile away the hours. Having said that, I've got time. I have hobbies: I'm getting pretty good at crocheting, and I'm nearly done with my celebratory Henry Rollins throw pillow. I've got my rocking chair, because I'm old, and my coffee, because I'm an addict. I can keep myself occupied for the time being. But nothing is forever. Everything is finite. My fuse will burn to the bomb, and when I go off, none of you will want to be within a million miles of my explosion. You can all go on thinking this is all fun and games and it's just good ol' Uncle Corey ramping it up so I can make you all laugh. But facts are facts. If the populace doesn't restrict this pungent bullshit to the realms behind closed doors soon, I'm going to lose it.

Don't even get me fucking *started* on Santa-Con.

Like I said: Vesuvius ain't got shit on me.

CHAPTER 3

FLIGHT OF THE DUMBKOFFS

Close your eyes and let your imagination chomp down on this bastard scenario for a second—that is, if you can do so without wanting to claw your face off like the guy in *Poltergeist*. It'll sting a bit, but do your best. Lean back and visualize the following hypothetical situation.

The alarm goes off, but you sleep through it. From the depths of your unconscious you ponder why you even set it in the first place. After you've hammered the snooze button half a dozen times, you finally let the correct time slither into your understanding, cutting its way past the fuzz of your slumber. Then it hits you: YOU'RE RUNNING LATE. You're not *too* terribly late, but it's enough that you need to hurry your ass if you're going to be on time. Hurtling out of bed, you don't even shower—you just throw on some clothes that may or may not be clean, having passed a hasty sniff test with a groggy nose. Couple a nonchalant rubbing of deodorant on each pit with a haphazard attempt at brushing your teeth, and your olfactory camouflage is complete. You've now officially shaved some time off of your original schedule for the morning. Gathering your belongings, you drag your bags downstairs just in time to see your friend pull up, who has graciously offered to provide a ride that early in the a.m. You toss your luggage in his or her boot, hatch, or trunk, collapse into the passenger seat, and gently imply that he or she should take "the fastest way to get there." You did it. You're barely awake, you stink a little bit, and you're fairly certain you've forgotten at least three things that are vital to your trip. But you did it. Then it hits you: you still have to get through the fucking airport. That's the moment when you deflate like a blown-up condom and wonder why you planned this excursion in the first place.

It's frucking fuss-trating, isn't it? That confidence you earned by trimming two hours of planned prep into twenty minutes of panicked performance is effectively rendered moot by the knowledge that you will now have to maneuver through the maze of pure hell that is the experience of having to fly with other people. If you have never flown before—Jesus, even if you have never been inside an airport before—no matter how eloquently I speak or how descriptive I get, there is no way I can truly describe this eventual excruciating hindrance. You can only live it, then talk about it at some support group in a YMCA basement somewhere while you drink see-through coffee and sit in shitty plastic chairs designed to make it impossible to cross your legs comfortably. I don't know about you, but it's hard for me to share with survivors and peers when I can't get my crotch in an acceptable position.

It's an issue so prevalent that no matter where I'm going, I could set my watch to it. It is exacerbating, perplexing, vexing, and so disproportionate to the right way of thinking that it's a wonder I can think half the time. Out of all the industries of the world, it is *the* supreme example of shortsightedness and lack of common-sense thinking I have ever experienced, and I swear to fucking Christ that it starts as soon as you pull up to the curb out front. There is a literal exit of conventional problem solving, a total evacuation of togetherness, and an embrace of all things selfish, inconsiderate, and manipulative. You'd think I was describing a fight club or a coliseum ready for a battle of epic size. Nope—that's not even in the same ballpark as the address I'm about to dress down. Anyone who's ever had the displeasure of traveling abroad or in bounds can tell you with absurd detail just how sucky it is to trounce around your local airport, a place as diverse in its asinine ways as its clientele.

There are a number of airports all over the world, and I have been through a majority of them. I have been flying to and from work and home on a constant basis since I was twenty years old, nearly as much time as I have spent driving on my own or shitting in places other than the pants I happen to be wearing. I'm not bragging; I'm just saying: I fly a lot. It's important for you to understand this before I start to eviscerate the airline industry. I deal with these people and the morons who board their planes too often for my own good. I don't like it. Honestly, I feel sorry for the employees of the airports of the world. But I can't be bothered giving a shit about them right now. This is about *you*: the baboon-assed travelers of this softball called terra firma. This is about the painful experience of having to move through airports with the assholes of Earth.

This chapter isn't even about flying, even though there are a host of problems that come once you actually board the plane. I've heard that at any given time there are at least one to four hundred *thousand* people in the air on jetliners en route to places around the globe. If only that number were higher, maybe I wouldn't bump into drill holes on a revolving basis. This, however, isn't the issue at hand. The issues occur in the hubs, code for the cities that the various airlines use as bases of operations. The issue is the behaviors I have to suffer through before you butt fucks even board the equipment, and I'm pissed to say that this list is extensive. In retro, it's a fascinating anthropological discovery that can be summed up in four phases: Me-Me-Me, WTF, Where Am I, and Hurry Up. These are the stages of air travel that have presented themselves over the last twenty years, predating 9/11, the popularity and availability of the Internet, cell phones and smartphones, and buckwheat neck pillows. But these incapacities of thought have certainly been made even more painful because of where we are now.

Me-Me-Me isn't the worst on the list, but it pisses me off almost as badly because it happens right out of the gate and sets the tone for your time in the terminals. You can feel it even before you pull up to unload: a general mass of troglodytes jockeying for a temporary parking space in front of a federal building where you can't smoke within twenty-five feet of the entrance. Cops swarm the sidewalks, making sure you're not there for very long, clipping hugs, handshakes, and good-bye kisses to nothing more than high fives and pecks on the cheek. It also seems like there's always one taxi driver who doesn't give a drippy shit about the flow of traffic, putting it in "park" directly in the middle of the third lane and tossing someone's luggage over Toyotas to land by the wayside. With a bit of luck and a favor owed to Allah, you finally find a sliver of concrete and slide in quickly. One awkward speedy exchange with your transport later and the dance of the damned begins. First things first, you have to get inside. This activity is stymied by a group of folks who seem as if they have never seen a revolving door before. This is the first signal that Me-Me-Me is in full view: not giving a wet tickle about anyone behind you. It's also a precursor to the pain that is Where Am I, because if you can't figure out a technological advancement as significant as a fucking door, there's no hope for you and you should be euthanized.

By hook or by crook, you get inside to the ticketing area. Me-Me-Me is now in full effect, and it presents itself in an experience that is akin to having a razorblade slide slowly across your hacky sack: the line to the ticket counter. Yes, it doesn't seem as laborious when it's written down. The reality is, unfortunately, the exact opposite. The ticket line has become a snaking mound of ill will, like waiting too long for the worst Disneyland ride ever created. Everyone in this line is mad as hell, and the strange thing is that the farther ahead you are in this line, the madder you get. The mindset is "I should *be* at the counter by now!" This is classic Me-Me-Me: your self-importance mounts as you get closer to your turn to get your boarding passes. Now, common sense should let you know that this is only the first step in a strenuous process leading to actually getting on the plane. But this isn't the case. The impatience levels reach such lethal numbers that I have witnessed sixty-year-old women scream at little kids who don't get out of their way fast enough. It's insane.

Another sign that you are in a line full of crazy assholes is the venom spat at people who don't get their bags around the corners of this Disney queue quick enough. That's space that could be taken up by another person, therefore moving you closer to the counter! To quote Magenta: SHIFT IT! You can tell from my rancor that I am indeed one of those pricks who bitch about this very practice. Those responsible for this are almost always the men and women who are going to beat the system by carrying on a suitcase that is clearly "checked bag" size. They drag this monstrosity behind them, knowing full well it's the size of an ancient steamer trunk equipped with wheels that can barely handle the weight of whatever's inside. But then they stand at the corners of the line like they're not sure whether they should keep going or not, as if at any moment they're going to change their minds about the trip and their excessive cargo. After a festering bundle of seconds that feels like hours, they finally lumber forward with a vacuous stare and a shuffling gait. I got to be honest here: it's enough to make me want to stab a motherfucker with a ballpoint pen, another vague hint at the Where Am I that lies just beyond the metal detectors.

Finally you reach the first trial: the ticket counter. Now, I've never been one to challenge the authority of the men and women who stand vigilant behind that counter, doling out tickets and bag tags like sentinels with printers, scarves, and individual name plates. But that does not mean that I haven't heard other travelers ripping into these people like kids on Christmas morning. This is where Me-Me-Me really comes into view. No matter what these people have done online, over the phone, through intermediaries, or what not, nothing makes sense now and everything has to been redone . . . *immediately*. Seat assignment? Change it. A checked bag that wasn't part of the original reservation? Add it and they're not paying for it. A carry-on bag that is the size of a Mini Cooper? It'll fit under their seat, they've flown with it a million times, and they refuse to check it. You got a problem with that? Get your manager over here; they want to register a complaint. People who work the ticket counter are in a no-win situation 99 percent of the time. In the past this might have been terms for suicide or at least a bit of disgruntled payback. But after 9/11 the power has shifted to the staff. Go ahead—run your mouth. You'll find yourself on the no-fly list faster than you can inhale cool air for a hot-winded retort.

If you manage to get past this labyrinth of rabid hostility, it's then a race to get to the security line—that is, if you're not heading outside for that last-minute cigarette at an illegal distance from their front door. Now, the security line is where things start to get interesting. The transition from Me-Me-Me to WTF begins here, amongst your fellow jetsetters and chart hoppers. It's like searching for a clean drink while wading through brackish waters: you never know what you're going to taste with each step of the way. You get the self-absorption, sure, but you also get the crushing reduction of brain cells as well. People can't figure out whether they're in a hurry or whether they have a clue to where they're going or even why they're going there to begin with. You eventually get to the front, TSA checks your credentials, and you make your way to the second trial: the detectors. This is, regretfully, where the "joy" of WTF begins.

Back in the line marching toward security clearance there appears to be a general emptying of the intellectual bowels, like a frightened person making pee-pee in the pants region. Brainiacs become dullards in the blink of an eye. Suddenly something as simple as showing your driver's license or passport to an official becomes a desperate search of every pocket while blinking uncontrollably. Even if you have your ticket and your ID in your hand, people who normally have a firm grasp of how NEXT IN LINE works now falter and pause, unsure whether it's their turn to go. I've seen virgins more self-assured while fumbling at three-hook bras. This culminates in the stupidity of the metal detectors and other more advanced booths of their kind. Trouble is, they have to sort out their shit at the assembly line to the X-ray machine first. This is a problem because apparently it's the first time for everyone standing there.

In their defense, countries all over the world have slightly different variations on the rules of this engagement. Some places are shoes on, and others are shoes off. Some lands give not one hot fiery fuck for iPads and stuff; others advise you to remove them and leave them behind for your loved ones to retrieve. However,

America is virtually unchanged in the last decade: shoes, belts, and jewelry off; computer out; no liquids; no toiletries over three ounces without a plastic bag; and empty your pockets of all the garbage you've been collecting since you arrived at the airport. This is standard procedure. Not only that, but there are security officers screaming these things in your face at different volumes and various ways while you're standing there. It's not fucking rocket science: it's all *right there*—on all the signs, on everyone's breath and minds . . . it's all right there. And like David Copperfield—the magic one, not the Dickens one—turning the Statue of Liberty into unblocked sky, this knowledge vanishes. What is left in its place appears to be a person who has about as much use as a door with no handles or hinges. Do you know what a door like that is called? A wall—hence the saying "dumber than a brick wall."

It begins with a slow, cautious spinning-head routine, casting empty looks around like a clumsy attempt to cheat from another student's test answers. If you're lucky, someone else pulls his or her belt off in plain sight so you do that, hastily trying to keep up. None of this matters, of course: someone always forgets something major on the list. They walk into the metal detector with a pocket full of laundry change and a wristwatch. They push their bags through the X-ray, loaded with their computers and three half-full bottles of soda. Coats come off . . . then go back on. Then the coats come back off, get wadded up, and are stuffed into the same bin as the computer. After security cautions them against this, they then place the coat with their shoes. But now they have to sort out their bags. This process is repeated with each person who gets to the conveyor belt. God forbid you get behind a family with more than one kid. By the time they have shoved everything and everyone through the machines, you've missed your flight and you should just go home. It's repulsive. Here's a piece of serious advice for anyone who clogs the throughways for the rest of us: if you've never flown before, take a bus.

With any bit of luck, you finally get through and to the other side, the gates, and the shops. Welcome to the most expensive convenience stores in the world. This has been a source of contention for everyone I know and every comedian on the planet who dares to rip open this tried and true mine of punitive gold. The prices in these newsstands, bookshops, and tiny markets are unbelievable, and that's on a good day with a fistful of twenties. Plus, there's a part of me that wonders why there are so many types of clothing for sale in the terminal stores. The sports tees and hats, I comprehend; souvenirs have been shilled since pharaohs offered parting pyramids to camel riders on the go. But suits? Cashmere sweaters? Dressy shoes and ties? Dresses and skirts and scarves (oh my)? When the hell did this become commerce for shit heels just passing through? Who in the sweet shit is showing up at the airport naked? I have never found myself in the market for a new suit of clothes while on a layover, no matter how fucking far I am flying. And even when I was drinking, I was never in need of a giant bottle of whiskey the size of a spare tire. How about this: instead of all these designer clothing stores and Worlds of Whiskeys, how about a fucking smoking lounge or two? DADDY NEEDS HIS FIX, YOU FuckERS!

Ahem . . . sorry.

Anyway, one $12 coffee, a pair of neon-green dress socks, and a bag of stale Chex Mix later, you can now start looking for your gate. But you should know better—it's not that simple. Before any of that shit can happen, you have Where Am I to deal with. Simply put, Where Am I is a minefield of dickheads who are wandering around *slowly*, with no idea where the hell they are or where they are going . . . and they're always in front of *me*. I have never wanted to kick old people so hard in my life. I have never felt such vile, bitter hatred for couples in matching Adidas gear before, and rarely does it come up outside of airports. There was that lovely husband and wife from Manchester who nearly ran me over with their Razor scooters, but that might have been my fault: I was on a bender eight years ago and had one of my own shoes off, brandishing it in an effort to fight off invisible beasts while they were trying to get by me. To Mr. and Mrs. Appleston, I sincerely apologize once again, and I do hope you've gotten the sight back in your respective eyes. Let's hear it for the Applestons! By the way, guys, I did end up slaying that Smaug-like bastard.

Where Am I is akin to searching for an address on a dark night on a street you've never been down before. You power down to a crawl, oblivious and squinty, trying in earnest to discover what the hell it really is you're looking for. Meanwhile, directly behind you, there is a pedestrian traffic jam stretching back to the exit sign by the family toilets. The thing is, there seems to be no way to get around people like you; every time we try to pass, your body, your suitcase, or both moves to block the fast lane that leads us to freedom. I believe those people afflicted with Where Am I have an unconscious reverse sensor, like a backup camera on a Range Rover, that disallows anyone from getting by. These people swallow up the hallway like a binge-eating Pac-Man, dedicated to making sure NONE SHALL PASS. Like the Black Knight, even if you try to cut off their legs and arms, they're still going to ruin your days and ways. It's times like this when I wish I was carrying a riot gun with plastic bullets, but they make you keep that in your checked luggage, so no joy. I assured them it was three ounces . . .

Because of the aggravating onset of Where Am I, I have been forced to apply an extra twenty minutes to my trip, either in the front end or the aftermath. Trust me: I can shuck and jive with the best of them, and it's still everything in my power to get around and away from these lost and lonely imbeciles who are bound and determined to make everyone wait as long as humanly possible. But thankfully I have been blessed with four speeds when walking through the airport: low, mid, high, and Fuck Off. Once I've throttled up to Fuck Off, I shoot by these insipid turds with a blast of motion and some pounding of the quads. It's everything in my power not to hurl insults over my shoulder like verbal Molotov cocktails at a riot after a GnR concert. This madness happens all over the fucking world, and it's absolutely intolerable. I'm going to have giant spinning blades attached to my Metallica *Kill 'Em All* Vans like the ones from *Death Race 2000* so I can start drilling into cocksuckers who refuse to do more than the speed of pulse.

Then again, Where Am I seems to have a temporary status. Once the culprits reach their gates, this diabolical mindset evaporates, leaving these travelers scratching their heads and consulting each other to figure out how exactly they'd gotten there. WAI seems to have the effects of a date-rape drug: no recollection of what happened and a slightly soiled feeling of violation when you do come back down to Earth. Maybe this is why suddenly it is now time for urgency. Standing at the counter and banging on the top, these wayward fuck tits now are in a state of furious panic and absolute selfish insistence. No one can go fast enough for their taste, and, worse still, once the doors open for the jet bridge, they transform into the embodiment of impatience, staring anyone in front of them down like a boxer with a gun. Anyone wearing a uniform also gets the gas. All of this anger means we've crossed the border from Where Am I into the cantankerous lands and minefields of Hurry Up.

Hurry Up is an interesting development because it's an amalgam of extraordinary scale: the selfishness of Me-Me-Me, the bewilderment of WTF, and the vacancy of Where Am I converge to create a tsunami rife with ego and vacuous thought. It's also completely fucking contrite: Why are you in such a fucking hurry to get on the damn plane? It's not leaving until we *all* get on it. It's not even going to begin taxiing until we're all strapped into our seats. What is your fucking damage? Do you seriously believe that once you've jammed yourself down into one of *the* most uncomfortable and unforgiving seats ever invented by Man, the pilot is going to swing his head around and start the final checklist so they can get into the air faster? Do you think your presence on the plane has *any* bearing on the scheduled departure? The answer is simple: F no. If you're not in your seat, they'll probably just stuff someone else into it. The flight attendants do a final walk-through before takeoff, counting what they call SOB, which stands for Souls on Board. This includes pilots, attendants, and passengers. I can guarantee you every day for the rest of my life and yours that number will always be bigger than one, meaning you.

This fact still doesn't keep people from corralling around the carpet outlining the entrance to the jet bridge, bunched together like refugees hoping for an extra ham sandwich to split with the kids. They pace in tiny little semicircles, waiting for their group to be called for boarding. Every time a group number is announced that isn't theirs, they groan, moan, and roll their eyes like teenagers listening to a lecture from their parents. They grip their tickets hard, soaking them in palm sweat. Their teeth grind so loud, I swear I can hear them all from here on my couch. The septic feeling is so powerful, it's quite hellish. Nobody cares about anyone else; in fact, if there were no rhyme or reason to the boarding process, people would get trampled like grandmothers in the eighties looking for an affordable Cabbage Patch Kid. It is truly vicious, this vitriol spewing from the faces of the visiting public. That's why I believe, in order for travelers to come back to a state of enjoyment while flying, TSA should offer blowjobs and/ or jellyrolls to everyone right at the curb.

You're laughing at me right now. That's fine. Genius is often scoffed at when it arrives in the form of odd choices and foreign advice. But I want you to think *hard* (snicker) about this idea for just a split second. Put yourself in the relaxation that accompanies a massive orgasm. Now imagine that feeling sticking with you all the while as you traverse the airport toward your gate. That knowing smile plastered on your face would let all those around you know everything was going to be okay. Take your time fishing your computer out of your satchel! Please, go ahead—I don't mind! No, no . . . after you! My turn to get on the plane? It's all good—we're all going to the same place! We're all family here! God, how good was *your* blowjob, mate? I know! Your wife got a vigorous rubbing as well? Brilliant! The *vibrations* (snicker) given off by that sort of stress reliever would cascade over everyone like a blanket, smoke, and a pancake. You know those little kiosks where they offer to shine your shoes or give you a massage? Fuck foot rubs—unless we're talking about a toe job. Then it would be a foot fuck rub.

Traveling shouldn't be this stressful. Fucking hell—*nothing* should be this stressful, not even a rectal exam or a body-cavity search. I blame the stupidity rampant in our civilization. You see, I believe that in order to be truly stupid, you have to have the smarts there to begin with. This intensifies the feeling when you've done something so daft, people stare at you with open disdain. Here lies the separation of stupidity and incompetence.

If you're stupid, you just didn't understand what happened and then make adjustments. If you're incompetent, you never bothered to learn in the first place. So the incompetent man keeps doing dumb shit even after he's cautioned not to. A stupid man can learn. An incompetent man cannot. So by that rationale, stupid people traveling abroad can be taught to figure it out. But why aren't you? You're not all incompetent; you managed to dress yourself in clothes that weren't covered in sick and boogies. What's the fucking deal, people?

I believe the glamour of flight has something to do with it. You see, years ago it was a luxury to fly on an airplane. People, dressed to the nines in their spats, suits, and fedoras, boarded a flight and were treated to the cutting edge of prestige. Now, with more equipment available and competitive pricing (kind of) it's more accessible to the general public to hop a puddle jumper and head off into the sunset. This, however, means that everyone can get in the act, and I do mean *everyone*. Shit cakes dressed like off-duty strippers show up to check in while draped in sweat pants and shitty college T-shirts—colleges they never went to, by the way—and meander through the airport like there are several sticks crammed up their tight, pink, bleached assholes. The importance of what they are about to get up to is completely gone. That means, to me, for the good of the airline industry, the only way to dispose of this ignorant rubbish is to jack the prices back up into the high stratosphere. Then again, come to think of it, most rich folk are about as well mannered as a batch of Tasmanian devils dressed in Gucci claw covers. The wealthy would just use this as another way to look down on us. Well . . . you. I can afford to fly anytime. But I'm no fuckin' rat! I guess until I can convince the government to implement my Curbside Fuck System, we'll all just have to get used to the fact that nearly every airport is a harbor for the equivalent of Greyhound buses fitted with wings that may or may not fall off in flight.

I'm going to be straight up with you: I fucking despise flying. I'm not afraid of flying, not even close. In fact, much like my wife, one of the few things I truly enjoy about being on an airplane is that no one can reach me while I'm in the air. No e-mails from people wanting something. No phone calls that will piss me off. Nobody can drop by unexpectedly or unannounced to bother me while I try to relax. It's just me, my wife, and a book I've been dying to read. With the exception of not being able to smoke and an odd aversion to pooping in the vacuum of the toilet, I cherish my time onboard. But the pros of this scenario are ground into dust under the weight of the cons I've discussed previously. Not only that, but I hate layovers so much that I once missed an entire tour on purpose because it was going to take me five layovers in different countries just to make it to the first concert. Go ahead—scoff at me all you want. I regret nothing.

Shall I describe to you how much I detest the flying experience? All right then . . .

I once had to fly home from the end of a Stone Sour tour in England. Now, although I have nothing against long flights, I am loathe to say I abhor long stays in airports while I wait to actually get the fuck out of Dodge and get home, especially with the implementation of "the nonsmoking terminals." Most airports, even international, are a bit shit to get through, and yet it's still fairly simple to get outside to have a smoke. This is *not* the case with London Heathrow Airport. Not only is it designed to give the flyer a migraine because of the twisting caverns and miles to go before you get to your gate, but it is also damn near impossible to get out, have a square, and get back in through security by the end of the week, much less by the time your flight takes off.

So once you're in Heathrow, *you are in*. So addicts like myself stand outside right up until the point at which you have to barrel inside, crush through customs, and catch the only flight home that leaves for hours. This, however, is only the beginning.

I have been forced to wander that airport for hours . . . and hours . . . and hours on end. The fucked thing is that I'm almost always stuck behind a vacationing couple from Geneva who cannot comprehend that there is essentially a mall inside this airport, so they stop to look at *everything*. Nine times out of ten, they stop right in front of me. The conversation is always the same and never interesting.

"Myrtle?"

"Yes, Heinrich?"

"Have you *seen* the size of this cheese wheel?"

"Oh my! That *is* big!"

"I know, I mean, my *goodness*! Who's going to eat that much cheese?"

"Well, it could be a present for someone!"

"A present? Of cheese? What kind of family is it?"

"How would I know, Heinrich?"

"I suppose they *could* be Russian . . . "

"Now, why's that?"

"Well, the state doesn't regulate their dairy consumption anymore, do they?"

" . . . Did they *ever* do that?"

"How should I know, Myrtle? I'm no commie!"

"I *never* said you were . . . "

"Okay then . . . "

After a few steps more, you'd hear:

"Myrtle?"

"Yes, Heinrich?"

"Have you *seen* the size of this boot-shaped whiskey bottle?"

"Oh *my*!"

The bitch about this scenario is that even though they have stopped, there is no way to get around this couple. They are just the right distance between the front of the shop and the oncoming foot traffic moving in the opposite direction. So it's like being stuck at stoplights that are talking to each other, having the most pointless conversation since the advent of self-government. This is hell in comfortable shoes. This is what happens when time becomes irrelevant: you talk to your mate about the need for giant wheels of cheddar and novelty whiskey flasks. This is me not giving a fuck; I'm just fucking trying to get home.

Heathrow, unfortunately, makes you earn that trip. No matter where you're going, domestic or foreign, you have to take a series of buses and trams to get there, and that's *after* you've gotten through passport control. I don't care what the actual specs on that airport are; it will never convince me that it is smaller than a city unto itself. Someone once showed me how London proper is actually only one square mile in diameter. Heathrow feels like it's at least one hundred times that size. Even as you get off the trains, trams, and buses, there is still quite a trek just to get to the gate. Then there's a good chance you'll have to go through a sort of security check *again*. What in the actual flying fuck is going on? I'm going to Iowa through New York—I'm not going to space through the queen's bung chute. Really? Is this fucking necessary? You're right: there is a great chance I'll be able to fashion a weapon using my colon and a wooden spoon I got from a sample of Ben and Jerry's ice cream. There, you fucking happy now? Can I just get on the plane so I can pass out and wake up at home? Cool—I'll just go fuck myself. Mahalo!

As you can see, I am no stranger to the pitfalls of Me-Me-Me, WTF, Where Am I, and Hurry Up. I get just as impatient, act just as ignorant, and become just as impossible as the global tribe and their mad dash from point A to point B. The straight line isn't good enough; there should be a million horsepower shoved into it. I find myself cutting paths through the people, mad and miserable, ready for a fight yet scared to death of doing so because as much as I hate everyone in that moment, I hate the idea of being stuck in the airport jail abroad even more. Trust me: the airport does in fact have a jail. I have a friend who ended up getting arrested and stuck behind aviation bars because he got wasted at like 8 a.m. and started some shit at the bar.

Let's talk about that for a minute: the overwhelming need many people have to imbibe gallons of alcohol—no matter what time it is—before, during, and after takeoff. It's like nobody gives a shit anymore about civility. If they are past security and their passport has been stamped, they are *officially* on vacation, and they are going to stay bombed to fuckin' bejeezus right up until they show up for work a week later. Now not only are you trying to get around dick bags so you can get home, but you're also avoiding drunken idiots who think American troops enforce the English language in other countries. They also think that every racist joke and ridiculous insight about international ways is hilarious to everyone. They must think that: they scream the shit loud enough so everyone can hear it and be embarrassed about it. Plus, with all the booze they're chugging down there's a very good chance they'll wake up in a Build-A-Bear Workshop, naked and balls deep in a container full of cotton and tiny bear panties. Yep. That's my people . . .

God, I fuckin' hate people.

I have dreams of making millions of dollars some day, hopefully in the not-so-distant future, and I'll let you in on the first fucking thing I am going to do. No, I'm not going to buy an island, although that is indeed high on my wish list. Oh, my first badass purchase is more practical than you realize. The first thing I'm going to do is buy a private jet. I know: it's a very "nouveau riche" thing to do, what with all the scabs like Justin fuckin' Bieber rolling that way. That cum wipe only moves that way so people can see him as opulent and worthy of envy. This is all well and good, seeing as his talent has an expiration date just short of curdled milk. Don't ask me to care about him—to me, he's a terrible person who deserves your adulation about as much as George W. Bush deserves a presidential library. With as much auto tuning that goes into his "singing," it's almost amazing he can talk to people without someone fixing his words in a fucking studio. But we'll get to him later . . . with relish.

You might be asking yourself, "Then why do you want a private jet? Do you really want any comparisons to those skin tags?" Honestly? I don't really give a shit because here's the thing: I don't plan on showing it off to anyone for anything. If I have my way, no one would even know I have one. The only people who would be savvy to this extravagance would be my wife and our immediate family—because no one is going to use it but us. I fly more every year than most families fly in their lifetimes. So if I could have my own jet, just like I own my own car: GOOD-BYE, AIRPORTS. SAYONARA, COMMERCIAL FLIGHTS. BEAT IT, ECONOMY CLASS.

Hello, private terminals and minimal delays.

I won't have to deal with the smashing, the smushing, the ramming and the cramming, the arguments and the impudence. No more cattle-rustling comparisons and no more half-assed attempts to tuck my severity back in my breeches when someone pisses me off. Out with the exasperation of exit signs to baggage claim and the trampling that occurs once you've deplaned and set your sights on what's next. All that will be left are the bare necessities: show up, drop your bags off, breeze through security, get on *your plane*, and get on your way. Planes aren't too expensive if you've got the liquid assets; it's the price of jet fuel that will knock your dick off. You think unleaded is pricey these days? Try working out how much juice you'll need for a G5, and I don't think they'll take just any credit card. Unless you're holding one of those nifty black AmEx cards—the ones my wife won't let me have yet—you might be hitchhiking into Aruba. But I won't care by then. I'll pawn all my shit and give a little bit more just to be able to avoid the crowds and stampedes at your friendly neighborhood public airport.

Sadly, until the day comes, I must consign myself to the Toxic Two-Step, snaking through the fuckers and trying not to kill everyone in a fit of white-hot fury. I have to pay the bills, and that means running the gamut to and from cities and principalities all over the world. I swallow bile and stow my carry-on while having to deal with these nitwits, for if airports are a Petri dish, then moronic behavior is the spore encrusted across its glassy surface. I guess we're all guilty when it comes to flying from portal to portal, and everything in my body wishes I could be okay with that. But the more I brush shoulders with you people, the more I either want to run like hell or fight like crazy. My only solace is that being dumb is not contagious. If it were, I'd be rocking the hospital masks like everyone in Tokyo. Maybe that's why so many of the Japanese wear those: they've been able to prove that the idiocy of foreigners can pass to one another and they won't take any chances. Fuck the pollution; fight the delusion. Hey, it makes sense to me. I've seen men and women in airports try to bathe themselves using drinking fountains. Are you telling me it doesn't scare you that *that* might be contagious?

The wells might have gone dry on the human race. Airports are a vision of what might be, a glimpse into a future when our rulers or heads of government are the ones who only throw their own shit when foreign dignitaries are in town and, only then, when they are saluting these ambassadors. We might see a time when you buy a car either for driving it or fucking it—or both if you can be bothered to think practically. Devo called this shit years ago when they sang about "Devolution "and "Mongoloid." Are we not men? Are we not devolving? If you've spent any time on YouTube or watching *Tosh.o*, you'll figure out that bands like Devo are actually more like a modern-day Nostradamus than you'd like to admit. When that day comes, when we are nothing more than monkeys in designer jeans and ball gags just looking for another shiny ass to follow in contempt, it won't seem like such a chore to go to places like the airport. Then again, airports might just be museums by then: a look into the past at a time when we as humans once had the faculties not only to control complicated machinery but also to fly. The bitch of it is . . . we'll still be bitching about the wait in line.

We're fucked. Enjoy your flight.

CHAPTER 4

DYSFUNCTION OVER FASHION

As I write this, I'm forty-one years of age (made official on December 8, 2014) and it's quite invigorating to me how incredibly hostile I am becoming as the time peels a little more off my impeccable sense of patience. Seriously—I am a fucking war machine with bushy eyebrows and half a pack of cigarettes. I snap as the crow flies and the wind blows, and frankly I don't really give a slick shit. The wife does, surely; she gives me the "Really, asshole?" look when I've crossed a line or I've gone on a wonderfully vile rant about the tiniest piece of stupidity I just happen to have noticed. So I am coming into my own with the whole Grumpy Old Man thing, and as you'll read below, it's getting easier for me to snap from one Slim Jim tangent to the next. Prepare to tear into the fucking spice.

On a fairly innocuous evening in 2013 I was channel surfing on my couch, searching for something on TV that didn't suck. Much to my dismay and discomfort, nothing fit that particular description, so I went to what I call my "second string sense of taste"; in other words, I was prepared to settle for anything that didn't feature ice road truckers, "real housewives" from any state, cooking, dancing, reality TV "fighting," or a creature called "Honey Boo Boo." The pickings were slim, and I was on the verge of saying fuck it and reading a book when I stumbled on the 2013 *Billboard Music Awards*. The announcer said, "Performing tonight, Prince!" That was all I needed to hear. I dropped the remote control, mushed my second set of cheeks a little deeper into the upholstery, and prepared for a rare live treat from His Royal Badness. Long story short, Prince was amazing. He had an all-girl band that could smoke any other juxtaposed male set of wannabes from any state in the union, and he himself was just sexy enough to make me question my, ahem, system preferences. That was the good news. The bad news was I had to sit through a painful hour of the most torturous and hideous music known to man. I have done all I can to purge my mind and memory of that noise (which apparently sells a lot of fucking albums, sadly). But what I cannot get out of my brain are the various outfits these idiots draped themselves in that night.

I'm just going to fucking say it: Justin Bieber wears clothes that make him look like he shit his fucking pants. These sort of britches look like a sleeker version of the saggy gold foil ones MC Hammer used to rock when he was selling Diet Pepsi. This fact doesn't make them any more cool—they're dumb. And it looked like he didn't know how to walk or dance in them, because the little dipshit tripped and stumbled twice while he was onstage "singing" (read: lip-synching) and performing for a crowd that booed him—to my delight. Justin: between your massive sense of self-importance, your terrible attitude problem, and the way you treat your fans, you don't deserve your fame. Take your fucking toys and go home; I promise we won't miss you. While you're at it, stick that bucket you pissed in over your head so we don't have to see the painfully vacant look on your face anymore.

The rampant trend of sad fashion was everywhere. Taylor Swift was in another gown designed to make her look less tall and lanky while also undermining her visible overbite. A host of hipster douches were acting rather bored while also making sure their "thrown together" wardrobe was high end and noticeable. Most of them had hair like tarantulas reaching for their prey. Between that and all the hip-hop artists trying desperately to outdo each other's "electronic fashion" statements, it was a cluster ripe for the fucking. If these are the people leading us into the future of couture, I think I'd rather staple maple leaves to my junk and make my way through the world like a Nat Geo Wild star: forget *Naked and Afraid*; I would be "Nude and Ruthless." No need for the clothes—just give me the spear and see what happens.

Sometimes I think none of you have mirrors in your houses. And if you do, they are all lying to you or vice versa. I have watched the sea of fashion move wave after wave of chic debris onto our shores for years now. Some of the stuff has been cool. A small percentage is classic: no-nonsense, get-it-done, zero-frills functionality, and I like that. The rest, however, is a storm of ridiculousness that has no purpose other than to give super-skinny bitches a job and a reason for you to feel like shit about yourself. High Fashion is ironically apt in its title because you have to be HIGH AS Fuck to think any of that bullshit is cool or worth the money and hassle. It's designed for mannequins, which means it's off limits to 98 percent of the human population. It's pretentious, overly dramatic, and, more importantly, impractical in that it is not durable or appealing. And yet dildos with way too much money fuck each other over to have these opulent designers create looks for them. It all looks uncomfortable and depressing. You'd find better bargains at a K-Mart Blue-Light Special.

Let's stick with High Fashion for a while.

Every time I watch the Haute to Trot come sashaying down the model's runway, I get the sense that if IKEA or Pier 1 Imports made clothing, this is the shit they would foist upon us. I've seen it all—from too many feathers and not enough cuffs to glitter literally coming out the wazoo . . . of the men. Everything is brittle and glued together. It's a fucking surprise that any of it makes it past one long stride of the legs. But there they go, staring blankly ahead like a sexbot with smushy bits, hell bent on getting to the end of the ramp so they can stop, strike a pose, toss a fleetingly judgmental glance over one shoulder, then streak back to the curtain so they can be fitted for the *next* impossibly temporary outfit they will present on the catwalk. The upper 1 percent sit ringside like tourists at a prizefight, oohing and aahing at each delectable bit of thatch and patch, punctuating every slice of excitement with a final look of bored enthusiasm that translates on TV as "we're only really here to CNBC (see and be seen), so try not to stare as you're paying absolute attention to us."

What a load of bull fuck . . .

Never in my life have I seen anything on those runways that makes me want to wear it. Never in my dreams would I be caught dead in any of that shit. So why is it such a fascination for so many people who, on any other day, would scoff and mock right along with me? Those Bravo Network shows do *huge* business, so I know there's something crazy going on out there in TV Land. Is it because the stuff looks so dramatically foreign that it would be like dressing up to star in a play? Is it so people can feel like they're living out a Dr. Seuss fantasy of some sort? Am I reading too much into this? Should I take the tablets, Tiger? Did you get that last reference? Did you know I could juggle four chainsaws at once? Did I ever tell you about the time I lied to you all about being able to juggle four chainsaws at once? You remember that time I lied to you about juggling chainsaws? Am I rambling? Then why haven't you stopped me yet?

Let's get off the ramp and onto the street for a while. That's where the heart of real fashion comes from, the reservoir of inspiration and reality coming together to make a Reece's Cup full of tight-fitting kick ass. But I've found it sucks just as bad at sea level down here too. There is a remarkable phenomenon going on in the "Indie" scene in which men are tight-rolling their pant cuffs halfway up their calves, only to wear crappy dress shoes with no socks on. This, quite frankly, is a dick move. You all look like cunts. I'm sorry—I'm sure you were all very proud of yourselves for not only dressing on your own this morning but also putting a lot of thought and care into this pathetic ensemble, but as my British friends would say, "You really look a prick." And they wouldn't lie to us: they're British, therefore they do nothing wrong . . . unless you count the Spice Girls. But that was the nineties—nobody can *possibly* remember that far back. That's like trying to remember Thursday . . . good luck with that.

It's beyond me who comes up with these horrific ideas. I believe that somewhere in Miami there is a Masonic-like temple filled with bell-end fuck-ups with nothing better to do than send out the ugliest shit imaginable. Every six months these ball bags take turns spinning a giant Bingo drum full of worst-case fashion scenarios. They pick two—one for each coast, knowing that these ideas will slowly work their way inland, colliding in the Midwest, where trends go to die. By the time these ideas are "hot" in Des Moines, Iowa, the couture conspirators go back to the big spinning drum of shit and start it all over again. That's why fashion doesn't last long in the Heartland: if you can't wear it at work, we don't really give a shit. But New York and LA have never really cared about things like dress codes or wearing clothes that cover the bottoms of your ass lips. It's stuff like that that makes me happy Carrie never wore Crocs on *Sex and the City*: housewives all over Chicago would still be rocking that shit to this day, slurping cosmos out of old *Barbie and the Rockers* Thermoses on their way to get their nails done.

As I said before—or, more appropriately, "hinted at"—I am now forty-one. That means not only am I "seriously ancient," as my son, Griffin, has pronounced, but it also means I can remember trends that go back four decades . . . and that shit wasn't pretty. I was a sad participant—albeit an occasionally reluctant one—in the following: polyester, bell bottoms *and* flares, spandex, parachute pants, neon colors, aqua socks, JNCO jeans, wallet chains, silvery short-sleeved button-ups, tie-dyed *anything*, high waters, corduroys, *more* spandex, and pink. Just simply the color pink: yeah, I remember that, and I still have a T-shirt affirming that "Pink Is the New Black." Obviously that T-shirt was very mistaken. That doesn't mean it didn't happen. There are some things in life you'll have to accept: Corey Taylor had a mullet, wore shit clothes, and, at one time, adorned his body with the color pink.

I'm not proud of it. But I stand by my units.

I also remember weird fads like friendship pins: little safety pins with different colored tiny beads on them. In third grade that was the *rage*; people put them on their shoes and on the breasts of their shirts. If you didn't have one or no one had given you one, you were deemed a loser—quite harsh for kids under the age of ten. And kids *knew* if you made them yourself and put them on your own shoes. Kids are prescient when it comes to covert operations like pretending you have friends and have no proof of such relationships. These same people probably passed that trend on to their own kids in the form of friendship braids or bracelets. When those same children grow up, they will pass something on to *their* children, like friendship chastity belts (being a dad, that's not a bad idea . . .). These adults will then force their husbands to go to Jared's and put together obnoxious charm bracelets with stuff like hearts, footballs, and the Eiffel Tower on them . . . then pay way too much for said trinkets. Like I said, we're all stupid and none more than men when it comes to keeping members of the opposite sex happy—or at the very least to keep them from screaming at them in the car on the way home from dinner on their anniversary.

The last time I really gave a shit about looking cool was when I was fourteen. I still had very little money, and it was kind of a chore to find things that felt in style. My mother and her best friend came up with a solution that to this day makes me cringe: they took my mother's best friend's daughter's jeans and simply tailored them (no puns, please) to fit my scrawny ass. Yes, friends and enemies: for a full year of my life I wore women's jeans to school because I couldn't afford men's jeans of any kind. Was I ashamed? Duh. Did the other kids find out and fuck with me? Seeing as the other girls had the *same style jeans* as I did, that would be an emphatic "yes." Do I miss wearing women's clothing? Not really, because I wear them every chance I get. Might this be why I have a deep-seated hatred for fashion of any kind? Most likely, yes. Do I want to talk more about it? I'm sorry, but our time's up for today. But I feel like we've made some really important strides toward what the underlying problems are.

Lady Gaga wears meat suits and smears mascara on her face. The critics rave and call it art. Britney Spears shaves her head and starts wearing hoodies while doling out the accidental VJJ shots. People call her crazy. The Red Hot Chili Peppers go out on stage dressed as light bulbs and pose for photos wearing socks and nothing else. They are labeled cutting-edge frontrunners. JT and Ms. Jackson (if you're nasty) let a nip slip during a one-sided Super Bowl half-time show. Parents—well, at least the mothers—everywhere are appalled. Miley Cyrus plays on MTV in what can only be described as a bizarre anime circus stage show, complete with wrecking balls and uncomfortable twerking. Need I say more? I believe we're all on the same page about how fucking banana sandwich *that* little girl has turned out to be. It's like the more famous someone gets, the more their fashion radar goes awry and it's the Emperor's New Clothes in 3D, showing our idols for who and what they really are as they run ridiculously through the streets. We all follow along, but the kicker comes in the strangest form, because most of us might be mocking them, but the rest are taking notes and smartphone pictures so we can get the look right when we get home. Are we *that* fucking ignorant? The million-dollar answer is apparently, or else I wouldn't have this chapter in this book.

Look, we're humans. We are spectacular at being brilliant and buffoonish simultaneously. In fact, if Lenny Kravitz went on YouTube and told us all to paste palm fronds painted with iridescent moles onto our asses, every ball bag in a café on Manhattan Island would look green and eerily shiny the next day, and housewives up and down Rodeo Drive would be plunking down heavy plastic to buy and don what would essentially add up to an oversized disco salad. That's just how we roll. We chase trends like dogs chase cars. We bite into fads the way kids bite into taffy—with no regrets and no thought about what this will look and feel like in retrospect. I'm sure most hippies look back and sigh sadly, wishing they'd just stuck with the mod look of the early sixties instead of the floppy pant legs and scratchy threads of the later sixties. But when you're that fucking high, I suppose it's a wonder you remembered to get dressed at all. So we're all susceptible to fawning for shallow flattery. That doesn't mean we're not stupid for it.

When I was a kid, feathered hair and alligator-baited short sleeves were a rage. Women teased their hair as high as humanly possible, and the entire natural world seemed to be stone washed. I wasn't entirely impressed, but that doesn't mean I wasn't forced through peer pressure and social facilitation to engage in these atrocities. Yes, I wore that shit. But you need to understand that this was all that was available at the time. Thrift shops weren't the centers of the groovy universe like they are today. You couldn't get away with ironic fashion in the eighties—it was virtually extinct in those days. I am indeed aware of how fucking sad I sound right now. Shit happens in every industry. It was a tough time for people of my ilk: the sad few who were forced to commit the sins of terrible fashion faux pas. But it was either that or go to school in mechanic's uniforms, and after it didn't work the first time, I didn't do it again until my tenure in Slipknot began. So Plan B was a shitty bust.

Not all of the stuff was bad, though. I can remember being skinny and cool enough to wear punk/goth/metal/rock fashion pretty well. I had a considerable collection of bondage pants, poet shirts (yes, poet shirts—I was a Lestat fan . . .), leather jackets, and enough Iron Maiden Ts to stock a Hot Topic on Black Friday. Now, I couldn't pull most of this off today—I may not be fat, but I have a neck the size of an offensive lineman. However, I have a sense of pride that, among my pack of wild dogs, I could hang with the Dobermans. I couldn't tell you whether I looked worth a shit, but enough people took notice that I wasn't ostracized either. So maybe I did give a shit about fashion many aeons ago. But then I discovered flannels, jeans, and comfortable Vans. Effectively my life as a billboard was over.

As a (snicker) celebrity, I am encouraged by others to dress up from time to time, especially at awards shows. You can guess how those conversations go by the suits I have worn diligently to the Kerrang Awards for years. If you're not familiar, just Google "Moods of Norway," and that's just the tip to that titanic iceberg. Every once in a while, though, I do throw on a nice suit so the wife and I can go out and look respectable. I admit she looks much better than I do when it comes to the upper echelons of suave accoutrement. I just do my best to keep up while hoping I also don't make her look like she's married to a guy who still works at Hardee's. Unfortunately, for the most part, I just can't be bothered to give a shit. I've said it before and I'll say it again: when I wear a suit, I feel like I raided my uncle's closet. They just feel like someone else's clothes. I wish I were more comfortable in this stuff, but I used to streak naked around my old neighborhood, and I can honestly say I felt more normal doing that than wearing a tuxedo.

Maybe it's because of the way I have witnessed other people stress over how they look and the way they worry whether people are going to notice or, worse yet, make fun of them. Let's face it: Joan Rivers, God rest her soul, was ripping people to shreds over their fashion sense a lot longer than I was. I should have let her edit this chapter before she passed just to make sure I didn't step on any of her material. There was a malicious gaze of sheer glee that glazed over her as she picked over the clothes that people were wearing to places like the Oscars or the Grammys, like a kid watching his friends eat candy he *knows* fell in poop. You could almost see the targets in her eyes as the masses moved their asses through her crosshairs. When she found the weakest of the pack, she pounced. Rivers did *not* let up until her comments were in *People, Us Weekly,* and every website devoted to eating our heroes. Then a few months later it would happen again. I'm sorry, but I'd rather wear sweatpants into the White House with the world's biggest boner than go through *that* kind of scrutiny any time in my fucking future.

It's also my distaste for "peacocking" that causes me to turn my nose up at the deliverance of trendy getups. To me, alpha males are like the Betamax: not much use in the modern world and a pain in the ass to get rid of. Alpha *anything* is just ugly—women are just as bad. This brings me to the center of the universe where all this hellish crap collides: the modern-day club night. Good fucking God, I haven't experienced discomfort like this since my first rectal exam . . . and at least my doctor felt bad about it later. Let me explain—not about the rectal exam but about the . . . never mind. It would take longer to back out of this apology correctly than it would to explain why it's none of your business about that exam or why I'm depressed that my doctor hasn't called me.

One weird moan . . .

Anyway, I did a couple of solo shows in Las Vegas a few years back—one with a band full of my friends and another one purely acoustic—and the show's promoters asked me to make an appearance at their club as a way to drum up excitement for the events. For whatever reason I agreed. Almost as a subliminal way of admitting that I'd made a huge error in judgment, I dragged my friends in the band and the rest of my family along with me. It became very apparent I'd made a horrible decision as I was suddenly and effectively blasted by nausea and regret once we entered the establishment.

Everywhere I looked men and women alike were gussied up in their "party clothes," which, by the way, ALL FuckING LOOK THE GODDAMN SAME, just in different colors and cuts. It was like being in the Realm of the Replicates on Hawaiian-Shirt Wednesday. The women all had on dresses that barely fit over their surgically enhanced bodies, making them resemble a strange mix of Madame Trousseau's and the Hall of Presidents at Disney. There was no room to dance, but they did their best to do so anyway, clumsily flailing and wailing in a room that was too small to be that loud. The men were, shall we say, afflicted with the same outfit: tight dress shirts with rolled sleeves, terrible jeans with bedazzled jewels and tribal stitching, heavily gelled spiky/slicked hair, and black nondescript shoes. Every one of them had already sweated right through their clothes. Every one of them looked greasy and moist. Every one of them smelled like they'd bathed in Cool Water or some other noxious tonic. It was by far the grossest display I've had to endure in my forty years of dragging knuckles on this planet, and that's saying something—I've been to Tijuana.

The music might as well have been cued up by the entire cast of the *Jersey Shore*. This did nothing to improve my situation; in fact, it made it harder for me to leave because everywhere I looked these mooks were "dancing." Dancing, as I like to say, like they were being shot with arrows. They were also blocking all the exits with their meandering moves and silly spillage. I had nowhere to go, so the family, my friends, and I huddled in a back booth, mocking the people while also studying their habits. The fucked up thing is that with the exception of a table of businessmen from Dallas, NOT ONE PERSON IN THE JOINT GAVE A SHIT THAT I WAS THERE.

Not one.

There was no real reason for me to be there—this wasn't exactly my demographic. But the club owners insisted I stay for a while because it would be good for my turnout. As it in fact turned out, none of those people came to either show, and I looked for their types in the audience really fucking hard. I even sniffed the air a few times from the stage hoping to get a whiff of that sad aftershave scent I'd been bombarded with in that club. No dice. So I was subjected to repugnance on a molecular level, which assaulted every sense I came equipped with, for absolutely no good goddamn reason whatsoever. I remain convinced that a chunk of my dignity stayed behind and died a terrifying and unpleasant death deep in the leathery cushioned bowels that night. At the very least it fled the scene, concerned that this type of punishment might be thrust upon it again, and no amount of photos on milk cartons or any poignant vignettes on *Unsolved Mysteries* will ever bring it back to Daddy. And it's all because of that club.

That fucking club . . .

I was there for two damn hours.

Fuck . . .

I guess I shouldn't bitch too much. I mean, after all, if this is what people are comfortable and happy wearing, then who am I to judge? That all makes sense—it really does. But I'm really good at tearing shit asunder. People ask me why I don't have my own reality show. It's because I would be sued within seconds of the first episode for defamation of character. I just don't give a shit. When I see something that's stupid, I say something. No one is safe—I look in the mirror and attack myself every morning. I have a system: wipe the eye boogers out from the corners, pick up and load the toothbrush with Crest, call myself a foul-mouthed cocksucker, brush, spit, and floss. I like routine. And you have to agree that some of the shit these people wear is pretty silly. I saw a singer in a band—I won't name which one, but it's the same one who cries after sex every time—wearing a trench coat that only had one arm. Make no mistake, I *stared* at that motherfucker. I asked him whether he'd done that himself—you know, to be different. Nope—he paid a designer WAY TOO MUCH MONEY to do it *for* him. The whole time I just kept saying the same thing in my head: Who do you think you are, fucking Neo? Go back to the Matrix . . . and fuck yourself while you're at it. I'd tell you who it was, but that fucking guy *would* sue me in a redheaded heartbeat. But if you're savvy, there's a clue in this book to whom it was. If you guess it correctly, hit me up on Twitter: @Corey TaylorRock. You will win . . . fuck all.

Sometimes fashion does make things easier. There's no painful guesswork in school about which crowd you're going to hang out with—you look for the appropriate look. You can tell the grits from the preps from the geeks from the artists. You can find the Jocks among the goths, the heshers, the cheerleaders, and the glee folk. When you're young and just trying to find your place in the crowd, sometimes having that extra visual as a heads-up is worth its weight in fool's gold. In the long run it might cause more pain than pleasure, but most of us just want to get through it so real life can start. It's a lot like a minimum-security jailhouse: you just want to do your time, get out, and get on with it. Besides, we all know that most of the cool clothing in high school is just a costume, a pseudo-camouflage designed to help you blend in to the rest of your surroundings. But some people need the rockets' red glare—those outfits that burn white hot in the moment only to be severely dated upon inspection of yearbooks at the reunion.

"Jesus Christ, Kelly! Is that you in study hall wearing Uggs and a sweater vest? What were you *thinking*?"

"Shut up, Jesse! Where is it? . . . *Yeah*! Here's one of you in a cashmere jumper with meat cleaver earrings! Don't think for a *second* that this was *ever* cool!"

I'd keep going with that exchange, but bile has filled the back of my throat and I don't like that, so I'm stopping.

Superiority and confidence: these two forces of human nature combine like an after-school special with Captain Planet to reinforce how miserable we all feel when we're young. This is another reason why humans are dipshits sometimes. Because we don't have a handle on our own feelings at that age, we couldn't care less about other people's feelings. So we belittle and berate until those people are broken and banished to the corners of the gym, just biding their time until graduation. Hopefully they make it that far. But bullying has reached an all-time hateful high these days. There are swarms of disturbed children just waiting to pounce on any and every weakness. They are giving into the baser side of malice, set for destruction and a craving for flesh. They wouldn't know what to do with compassion if it were sticking in their craws. These physical reverberations ricochet across the years, doing damage no one can believe, all because someone dared to dress like a dick or because their family was poor and had to shop at Walmart.

There are savages among us who feel no empathy, and you got the obscene knack and bags to try to suggest to me we should give a fuck about what fucking clothes J-Lo is wearing? How about you take a deep breath, hold it, then plunge your face into your own crotch at a violent speed and angle in the hopes you eventually fuck your own face off? Can you do that for me? You forgot to do that today.

By "you" I don't mean anyone reading this book. Remember, we're talking about the Faceless They—the shit heels just off camera who are busy doing the most injustice. No, not you—you are my peeps! We're all good. Those other fuckholes can go eat their young for all I care. See?! Fashion makes me P-I-S-T PISSED! I want to smash shit against bricks or walls or coconuts—COCONUTS ARE HARD AND THEY HURT A LOT! Fuck, I'm on a tangent again. That's what happens when you hate everything. But I don't hate you—remember that. I'll bring it up again later just in case.

Jerry Seinfeld did a bit that discussed when we would all end up in the one-design space suits of the future. I'm paraphrasing, but he said, "In every movie that is set in the future or in space, it appears we're all wearing the same silver one-piece jumpsuits." He never really gave an answer when he thought that would happen, but I've been thinking. Most of the Earth looks like a bunch of hard-ons in different clothing today. If we're all going to look like tool bags anyway, maybe we should all start dressing the same. Is that too bold a Communist statement to make? It's *in* the movies—and movies *never* lie—so why not just get to it? It would certainly alleviate some of my headaches. Your wardrobe budget would *plummet*. You'd be forced to remember people's names because we're all dressed alike. Maybe the differences that force us apart would become a nonissue, seeing as we'd all be in uniforms and there would be no assumptions about religion, class, or tax bracket.

But, of course, we're only human.

All it would take is one friendship pin on the lapel of your space suit.

One person at work will notice it and ask about it. The next day that person will come back with two friendship pins on. Then four people will come in covered in them. Within a week the pins would become bracelets. Within a month Macy's would be nut-deep in a Fall Friendship Sale. Paris would come up with a spring line for friendship chains that would tie people to each other. By year's end the friendship pins and bracelets would be obsolete. In their stead would be love knots, grievance flowers for collars, and malice tape that you would only wear at family reunions. Then the real revolution would begin. First we'd roll up the sleeves on our silver unitards. Then we'd tight-roll our already tight cuffs. Then we'd cut off the legs. Then we'd only cut off one arm (so stupid . . .). By the time two years had passed, people would be talking about why we were all in the same out-fits in the first place. There would be rallies and protests where we'd all show up wearing them inside out or upside down—any-thing to make our point. That's when the militia would come in. That's when the real fashion wars would drive us all toward the brink of oblivion.

It's our genetic code that fucks us in the end: we all need to be individuals, to stand out in the crowd, and to be heard in the convex confines of the herd. It's the price we pay for free will that keeps us apart and unwilling to read or, for that matter, be on the same page. Maybe this is why we're all destined to fight with one another for the rest of our existence. We'll never be able to get out of our own ways long enough to see the other's point of view because we're all so fucking busy paying more attention to the sounds of our own voices than to what the other person is saying. We're always more impressed with our retorts than the rest of the conversation. The whole time the opponent is talking we're just thinking about what we're going to say in reply; we don't even hear the other side of it. So if you think a thing like fashion couldn't start a war—if you believe that it's too big a jump from flares to full-blown chaos—think about this: unless you saw them Sieg Heil, do you think you could tell a Nazi from anyone else unless they were in uniform?

Fashion plays a bigger part in how we view the world than even I can imagine sometimes. I wouldn't know whether someone was a priest unless they had on the collar. I wouldn't know whether someone was a soldier unless they were in their fatigues. I wouldn't know whether someone was Jewish unless they were dressed in Hasidic garb. That may be good or bad; it all depends on how you look at it. What I take from this is that I don't assume someone is something they are not unless I ask them or unless I see them in the clothing that would suggest such. I prefer to ask them. But I also assume the worst if someone is dressed like a dickhead. That might keep me from getting to know someone who might otherwise be quite intelligent and kind. Fashion divides us on so many levels that it takes a while to really break things down. Yes, fashion is good for the individual to express his or her self. But it can be devastating in so many other ways as well.

Attractiveness: that's what it boils down to in the long run.

Whether it's plain old posturing or out and out snogging, we want to look our best when we're doing it. The signs of the times have taken us down some seriously depressing and dark byways in regard to what is considered cool and hip. Yet it is imperative for sexual ripeness that we feel good about our decisions pertaining to the need for pressing against the proverbial flesh. This is also true for homosexuality or whatever your taste is: nobody wants to wake up with the troll from the party who looked like shit. As long as that person had "it" going on, you can wash away your worries in the morning shower or until someone skips a period. No one's going to brag about a hookup that makes you want to hide under your bed for days. Fashion smoothes out the rough edges of our awkward attempts to get down. The sad part is that once you're in it, the clothes come off, so there's no getting around how weird your partner looks at the time, no matter how rad his or her clothing looks.

That could be a positive alternative: nudity. With nudity the only things you're judged on are . . . okay scratch that. Depending on the weather or the circumstances, nudity can paint you into a corner socially that could take years to claw yourself out of, and that's only after therapy and an address change. So what's a better idea? Fuck, this is frustrating. Maybe if I paid more attention to what passes and what fails, I could wax a little more ecstatic, but honestly I just can't be bothered to care about it. Who gives a shit whether those shoes don't go with that dress? Who cares whether that shirt doesn't match that waistcoat? Who really shares a plump fuck whether nobody wears waistcoats anymore or calls them waistcoats or whatever? There's that diabolical bit in our mammalian brain pockets that enjoys a bit of schadenfreude as they're tucked into the backgrounds of senior proms and dance halls, praying that the cool kids have a series of serious wardrobe malfunctions just as the slow numbers begin. We need it to balance the scale because, let's face it: some people *do* look incredible with or without clothes. Others need all the help they can get. But when things go wrong, ahhhh . . . that's when we're all equal citizens on England's mountain green.

In summation, fashion makes us idiots in so many ways and on so many levels that, quite frankly, I'm amazed someone hasn't presented a bill to Congress to outlaw this type of behavior. It cuts the crowd into little pieces, gives people control over others' feelings, makes us look like dick faces in retrospect, and brings to the surface envy and malevolence that is so palpable, we could flavor it and serve it over toast. Speaking for the world at large, none of us want to feel like shit, and we certainly don't want to feel like we *look* like shit. But most of us do, and it's because we've got our cultural noses stuffed up into the ass in front of us, regardless of whose ass it is or what they're doing with it. Some of these may be high and mighty, but most of them may in fact just be mighty high wipers, and when our brown noses come back from being turned up at everything, all we're going to taste is shit. Humble pie is a turd no one wants to sample on a cold day. But you know what? It's certainly a dose that some of these cretins could use more often.

Who cares how you look? Just do what I do: pretend you're a superhero and wear the same thing every day. It's not gross if it's considered a "uniform" *and* you can claim you fight crime! Seriously, how much can I know about fashion to get this worked up about it? I'm in Slipknot, the band that wears matching coveralls and masks. I'm not exactly getting blown up by top designers to walk the runways at their events. But I have taste. I have class. There are no *real* photos of my naked body on the Intro-Webs. I'm smarter than most, even as I'm shorter than others. I think my opinion on this matter has a little heft. You don't have to listen to me, of course. But if you use your mind for a second, if you dedicate your faculties to something other than Tweets and whistles, you might pick up on it. If you take the time to let the smoke clear your eyes, you'll see the mirrors doing what they do best: hiding the evidence and twisting reality. Once that's done, all you have to do is find the exit out of the Fun House. But don't look back—you may catch a glimpse of how long the queue is that's pushing and barging through the entrance. And knowing people the way I do, it'll take everything you've got not to hop back in line.

Be comfortable. Be original. Be careful what you wish for. There are times and places to look your best and there are also those days when "screw this" is a great mind-set to have. Personally I try to merge those days as much as possible. Sure, you could set your watch to my sense of style, but hey, somewhere between Jeff Goldblum in *The Fly* and Doc Severenson from *The Tonight Show*, The Great Big Mouth abides. I don't need leather or lace, silk or canvas, or anything that comes with an expiration date. When all is said and done, I can rock the crowd in pajama bottoms, a Slayer T-shirt, my Scot's golf cap, a *Star Wars* zip-up, and some checkerboard Cons. *Or* I can go all out and really try for something disturbing, like what I wore on Halloween at the Hammersmith Apollo six years ago.

Some of you remember. Don't make me do it again.

CHAPTER 5

DRIVING ME CRAZY

Use your fucking turn signals.

That's right: no build-up, no funny story, and no cool segue in which I save a puma from a blender that has suddenly become self-aware, *Terminator* style. We are diving directly into the deepest shit possible. It's so simple and yet it seriously causes me fits of all-consuming, homicidal rage. I have honestly *followed* people to wherever they are going—or as far as the madness sustains me. One time I pulled into the driveway behind a particularly inept fuckhole behind the wheel of a Chevy Cavalier as they parked in their garage; I only left when it looked like they were going to dial 911. Another time long ago—I don't remember the year but I remember it was December—I pulled a rage-brake so hard that I spun out in the middle of Valley West Drive. Luckily there was no one around to ram into—damnit . . . —but I was so angry that I forgot where the hell I was going in the first place. I couldn't even remember why I was on the west side of Des Moines to begin with. All I knew was that I really needed to pummel someone with the hood of my car. But see-ing as I couldn't do that, I sat perpendicular, blocking two lanes of traffic, gripping the faux-leather wrap of my steering wheel, biting back venom. Finally I just gave up my prior endeavor and instead went to the mall and bought action figures.

This is what your dumbass driving "skills" make me: a livid, forgetful collector—or hoarder, as my wife calls me—who has a tendency to fishtail in light snow at major suburban intersections.

All because you people can't do something simple like pull up or down on a thin plastic/metal stem protruding from the side of your steering wheel, *well* within reach of those stupid little hands of yours. For fuck ball's sake, its use and meaning for existing is in the name of the contraption itself! It's a *turn* signal. You use it when you are going to fucking *TURN*! Not after you've already turned, not seconds before you make the actual turn, not incorrectly when you panic because you realize you haven't signaled at all so you signal left but you're actually turning right, and for that matter not bothering to signal at all. You use it when you turn. That's why it's named a fucking *turn signal*. This isn't algebra. Shit, this isn't even pressure to write a fucking haiku. It's an example of only the most common of common-sense gestures.

I get it: you were too busy texting to pull on it. You were too busy turning to let me know you were doing so safely. You were too busy smearing Avon and mud on your face in an attempt to blend in with your "coworkers" to be bothered with that tawdry little function in your fucking Kia Sedona. Fine. But here's the thing: when you don't do something you are required to do for safety reasons while you are handling a motor vehicle, I don't care what side of the fucking car you are on. SIGNAL THAT YOU ARE TURNING. I will definitely ram a motherfucker to prove a point. And I know enough police officers who would agree with my reasons to get away with it.

As you might assume, this chapter is all about your garbage excuse for driving. Of course, you'll understand that I myself am not included in these infractions. I am an impeccable driver—not one accident in all my years of firing up Detroit engines for transportation. The weird thing is, according to *everyone* I know, I'm one of the worst drivers to be in a car with. How the fish dick fuck stick does *that* work? No accidents on my record, no crazy Evel Kneivel stunts, no rolling from the car as I drive it toward a building full of bad guys, and yet I am the one they won't get in a car with. You have got to be fucking kidding me. I know for a fact that some of these friends of mine have been in accidents that were *their* fault. I know for a fact that most of them have had their licenses revoked at *least* once in their lives. But I'm the big bad daddy long-legs scaring the children as blood flows red on the highway? Show me on the doll where that makes *any* sense . . .

There *were* a few little missteps: the speeding tickets, the parking tickets, the time I got pulled over and my car was searched because, and I quote, "You *look* like you take drugs, son. Of course I pulled you over." *That* guy was a judgmental prick, but I got even. I made him get a warrant to search my car—made him sit there and wait with me until the warrant got there. Then I made no attempt to help him as he pulled my car apart, looking for drugs he "knew were there." The officer who brought the warrant apologized to me. The other officer, who was older, tried to give me a ticket for speeding after the fact, but I contested it in court and won. The older cop was slapped with a warning for harassment. Nothing against any other member of the police, but if he's out there . . . fuck you very much, officer.

So yeah, I'm a perfect driver in my own head. But aren't we all? I think that's where the problem stems from: the fact that we all think we're great behind the wheel, kind of like how all guys think they're awesome in bed and how all women think they're fooling anyone when they say they don't talk with their friends about how we are in bed. This is Hakuna Matada in its purest form. It is what it is, as I am prone to say at any given time during the day. It's a lot like incompetence in a weird way. Someone who's incompetent doesn't *know* they're incompetent because they don't know what they don't know, and even when it's pointed out to them, they can either accept it or contest it with slang, slurs, and silly expletives. So yes, my furry friends: you all suck the butter stick at driving. But don't let it get you down, because it's a universal affliction.

Here's something else that chaps my chowder: check your fucking mirrors and blind spot before you change lanes or make a turn. Some people just meander over without even seeing whether they're clear. This is a case of "I'm the Only Driver on the Planet" syndrome. The turn signals go in that category too. But you know you're dealing with one of these creatures when you're tooling down the highway, doing fine with the car next to you . . . and suddenly you're nearly being forced off the road by the pseudo Mad Max wannabe in the other lane who didn't give a shit whether anybody was there or not. Then when they do realize that this is a public road and someone else is on it, they don't give you a look of attrition; they look at you like it was *your* fault, like you snuck up on them even though they were behind you. Awareness is three-fourths of the issue when it comes to good or bad driving; the other quarter involves knowing what the car is capable of. Here's a hint: it's big as shit and has been known to kill. Figure it the fuck out.

If the roads were Crash-Up Derby, I wouldn't give a square toss—I'd fly a plane and drop balloons full of feces on you as I cruised overhead. But the mean streets aren't supposed to be that mean. They are lines between points A and B—means to an end, the way through the maze. You'd think with the awareness that roads are options and driving is a commitment, this would be simple physics. However, it all gets jumbled. It appears that awareness of the road and driving is optional with little commitment. That's like forgetting to light a gas stove, sticking the turkey in, letting the house fill with gas, then firing up a cigarette.

Los Angeles can suck it when it comes to driving. Seriously.

That fucking city is packed with incredibly fucked drivers, every one of them oblivious, full of entitlement, and asking to get crushed under my wheels. It's not like New York, where driving is a challenge and you hold on for dear life. It may terrify you, but you respect it in the Big Apple—it's all about precision, timing, and speed. Oh, and a shitload of honking horns and screaming East Coast accents. I can back that shit all day. You know you're going to have to deal with some crazy shit, so you prepare, but at least you know everyone else feels the same way. This is not the case in California, where "depending on how the energy feels," an asshole in a Prius may not make a left turn all day because their chakras won't allow it. These people make turns from THE MIDDLE LANE; as far as I'm concerned, they *earn* the dents in their fucking cars.

I finally figured out why people in LA drive like shit—it's because they *walk* like shit. While I was making *.5: The Gray Chapter*, my wife and I were living in Venice. So I would go for runs on the boardwalk down by the beach. The upside to this was miles of twisting, turning, paved foot/bike paths, winding along the coastline and offering you a wonderful view of some of the good shit California has to offer. The downside was enough to make me want to run to the end of the Santa Monica pier and jump in with an armload of free weights to make sure I bottomed out and drowned completely. These tracks would be littered with people just meandering about, looking at the sand or the sky or the skate shops in the market areas. If you remember the airport chapter, you know my feelings on people who just train off at the brain and give the appearance that they were just released from a basement dungeon loaded with shellshock. The people on the boardwalk make those people look like they're running heated marathons. You try to run by them; they just casually get in your way. They *see* you coming they just think to themselves "fuck it" and spread out across the lanes like they are at a protest. Hey, Grandma! Get the Fuck out of my way! I don't give a shit that you're eighty-three—I made the mistake of eating Del Taco at four in the morning! I need to run this garbage off before I accidentally shit myself!

So the walking is reflected in their driving. You'll be following some jerk off in his or her Corolla, wishing death on them because they're cruising around at a healthy 23 mph, when suddenly their stupid brake lights come on, you nearly crush right into their ass end, and they begin the most painfully lackadaisical turn known to man or beast, not even using the turn signal until they are halfway through the intersection. No amount of honking, cursing, yelling, or gesturing of legal firearms can harsh their mellow. They didn't even realize it was their turn until they got right on top of it. It's times like these that make me wish I had a fucking flamethrower on hand.

Christ, I need to wipe my mouth: I'm frothing over here . . .

It's a miracle to me that I don't have more notches in my gun barrel. That's not me admitting that I have a gun with notches representing kills I may or may not be responsible for. "I have never killed anyone for being stupid." I used those marks to denote a quotation, and that could have come from *anybody*, really. So as far as *you* know, "I do not have a gun with notches representing kills I may or may not be responsible for" . . . said someone, somewhere most certainly.

Let's stay in California for a minute—if we really have to. Here's another issue on the road I fucking loathe: people in "high-end" cars who feel the need to rev them up and float in and out of traffic. Now, when I say high end I don't mean real high end, like your Ferraris, Porsches, Aston Martins, and whatnot. I mean Honda Accords with spoilers equipped with engines that sound like bored-out lawn mowers, complete with primer paint jobs and the giant window decal in Old English font that reads something *tough* like "REBEL" or "THUNDER." You know the cars I'm talking about. I can almost *guarantee* that we all make fun of these dickheads on a regular basis. They zip in and out of the flow on the road, thinking we are impressed. The only thing impressed on us is the fact that the driver is a ball bag with a license.

You may be getting the idea that I dislike driving. This is not the case at all! I love being behind the wheel, floating down the road at a healthy clip, music cranked, windows down, letting the breeze keep me posted on how fast I'm actually going. I love driving, especially on the highway. Where most people seem opposed to long road trips, I positively love them. I used to go on long trips all the time. The highway is close to being the last place where you can get out on the concrete and fly with no restrictions outside of the usual speed limits and regulations. But notice I said "close." I have to add this because of an affliction I call the "Left Lane Conspiracy." In Britain and other places where the driving is reversed, you may call it the "Right Lane

Conspiracy." But for now I'm going to describe it from an American perspective, so just convert on your own terms depending on where your life happens to hit the gas.

Everyone knows that on the highways, freeways, and interstates there is a generally accepted rule of thumb: the left lane is fast and the right lane is slow. Sure, you can debate that by saying, "Well, actually the left lane is meant to be a passing lane." Okay, well, that's the fast lane: it's so I can *pass* you. Just because I don't happen to leave that lane doesn't mean I can't use it for exactly what it's meant for. It's the fast lane—get over yourselves. Left lane = fast; right lane = slow. I can't begin to understand how anyone on the planet could miss that memo. Hell, I knew that before I could reach the fucking pedals. But apparently there are those who not only don't seem to understand this pseudo-factoid but also flat out refuse to acknowledge it. So much like a batch of elderly bridge club members moseying down the boardwalk in Venice, they flitter about the byways, abusing the left lane. Then, when you come up behind them, they ignore you. When you try to go around them using the right lane, which is a necessary evil sometimes, they speed up and try to match you. Only when you get back in the left lane behind them do they *slowly* proceed to change lanes, forgetting to use THAT FuckING TURN SIGNAL until the very last second. Then, as you pass by them in a fit of rage, they give you that shitty "tsk tsk" look. Sorry, Uncle Fuck Slick, but that is a surefire way of getting slammed into and run off the road, Mad Max style. You have the conceit to disregard the cherished Left Lane Rule, and you're going to judge *me*? I have friends who are police. I'll have them run your plates so I know where you live. Then I'll interrupt your dinner and we'll discuss your terrible decisions as I languidly pat a cricket bat in my hand.

Note to you and yours: don't fuck with the guy who's willing to go crazy to prove a point.

There's an addendum to this, however. If I'm in the fast lane with cars on my right side and you come flying up behind me expecting me to get over when there's clearly no way I can do so, *do not* flash your fucking lights at me. Yes, I know we're in the middle of nowhere and you're in a terrible hurry. But if I can't get over at that exact moment, settle the fuck down. I'm not going to force an Astro van full of Denver transplants off onto the shoulder just so you can get to Lawrence, Kansas, three minutes quicker. Wait until I get past the congestion, and *then* I'll get over for you. But if one more prick flashes his dumb halogen headlamps at me when there's nothing safely I can do, I *will* do something dangerous. I'll slam on my brakes and kill us both . . . just to be right. Again, just a gentle reminder: DO NOT Fuck WITH THE GUY WHO'S WILLING TO GO CRAZY TO PROVE A POINT.

Instructors and aficionados like to talk about offensive and defensive driving, the difference between maneuvering aggressively or passively. That's all well and good, but it doesn't really work in this day and age. We need more intelligence and awareness on the road, and you can't keep adding choices to people who aren't paying attention in the first place. So here's the deal: from now on there's only two ways to drive: offensively and offensively. Confused? Don't be. It simply comes due to pronunciation. Look at it this way: it's the difference between "aww-fensively" and "uhh-fensively." The former is really the original. It's aggressive, safe driving—knowing what your car can do and using it to its full potential. The latter is just what you imagine— coaxing your car around in a fit of dumb mumbling, "Uhhh . . . " So there it is. It's either offensively or offensively. Figure it out or get out of my fucking way.

I hate to say it, but I believe we may have reached an impregnable impasse here. The majority of the population sucks on a space-time vacuum level when it comes to operating a motor vehicle. So, as always, everyone can relax because I have the solution to our—well, *my*—problem. In a fit of genius, caffeine, and lack of anything good on television, I have come up with five new driving laws that, if they are implemented correctly, will solve a lot of issues out there in traffic. Now in *my* head these are all incredibly reasonable and in some cases necessary for the elimination of things like logjams and ridiculous fender benders. Just bear with me and hear me out before you fuckers go running to my wife or my Gram saying he's off his meds again and somebody needs to rein me in. Besides, we all know I stopped taking those pills years ago. That's how we got *here*.

Now . . . the extra laws!

New Law Number One: all cars will be equipped with new technology requiring all people to pass a simple IQ test in order to start their car.

You read that correctly. This is akin to the car lock systems with breathalyzers. You know the ones: someone gets too many DUIs—or DWIs, depending on where you live. These shit stains talk their way out of jail time or license suspension. So the courts make them apply breathalyzers to their smart keys for their cars so the cars won't start if they blow over the legal limit. Yeah, that seems like a *great* idea. Now you have streets full of drunken pedestrians instead of drunken drivers. What's next? Chastity belts equipped with breathalyzers for unfit mothers? Not to marginalize an issue like drunk driving, but those people should spend some time in a cell, not begging their sober friend (i.e., the one on antibiotics who couldn't drink that night anyway) to blow in their keys so they can get home. It doesn't even occur to them to just have that sober friend drive: it's not the booze that gets you in the end but the fucking stubbornness.

So it's a lot like that, but crossed with the driver's license electronic exam. With the help of Lumosity.com, we'll develop a key-lock in which the driver must answer at least 90 percent of the questions correctly for the key to work. The lock will have a random-question generator so it's different *every time*. Much like the written test in a driving exam, if you're not doing well and are not going to pass, the key will shut off automatically and you won't even be allowed to finish the test. Then you can't use your car for twenty-four hours. No, this is not another "liberal conspiracy." No, this is not another crippling example of "health and safety gone mad." This is to ensure that my blood pressure doesn't go through the fucking roof when I'm picking Griff up from school. It will also make you think not only when you're on the road but genuinely think about where you're going and for how long. I guarantee you LA will look like a fucking ghost town when my "intelli-key" is implemented. Maybe then I can get in my car and go somewhere in less than two fucking hours that's two miles away.

New Law Number Two: a person must show they are able to *handle* a high-performance car before they can legally buy one, whether that means driving it or keeping the keys safe from young adults.

This is for the guy in the Audi RS8 who's grinding gears and slowing everyone down, changing lanes without looking, and stalling out at the green light because they don't know how to drive a fucking clutch. This is also directed toward the son or daughter of someone with money driving "the family Dodge Viper" rather erratically and dangerously, going way too fast in a school zone without a care in the world because "my dad will get me out of any ticket the cops give me." Look, some cars are hard to drive correctly. They rev high, brake low, and kick ass in ways the average wheel handler just can't wrap their heads around. Just because you have money doesn't mean you can drive a hyper-car. Just because you can afford the new Aston Martin Vanquish doesn't mean you should buy one, especially if you have teenage kids. All it takes is one night away with your wife, and that same super-car has a very good chance of spending the rest of its existence rusting at the bottom of the local lake, all because "little Johnny wanted to show off for his friends and snuck it out while we were at *Les Miz*." So at high-end dealerships there must be a comprehensive track where potential buyers must show beyond a shadow of a doubt that they can handle the cars they are perusing. They must also prove with physical evidence and video footage that they are in possession of a safe that has been specifically designed to keep those keys out of the hands of little big shots who could potentially abuse their hard-fought right to have that car in the first place.

Follow-up: in order to have access to this special car, the teenager must be able to show and prove that they can pick up chicks (or dudes, to be fair) on their own, with no help from the car. Then and *only* then can there be an addendum placed on the service.

Are you digging the laws? You better—I put a lot of thought and effort into these. I don't just sit here in my pajammy-jams consumed with inane insanity for my health. But I do make it look good—especially with my plaid slippers. They tie every outfit together, like little Scottish pillows for Hugo and his friends. The slippers *do* leave a lot of lint in my toes. This is the price you pay for toe security. What would you rather have: little fluffs of willowy fibers or dirt and crud stuck in between your piggies? Seriously? Well, sorry if I come off all judgy, but that's just fuckin' weird.

I'm wandering again.

New Law Number Three: all cars must have tiny billboards on their roofs with the driver's face and name on it.

If you live in or have ever been to New York and other bigger metro cities, you will recognize in your mind the type of signage I am talking about because they adorn almost every cab and taxi on the roads in these places. If not, they are fairly triangular and usually have smeared on them some sort of ad for lawyers or nightclubs or even movie posters. So every car would have one of those, with your picture and at *least* your first name on it—no pertinent info or anything, just enough so we know who you are and can curse you by name instead of relying on a car horn to do a below-average job of that same thing for us. Honking my horn only says so much; I should be able to white-knuckle the steering wheel, grit my teeth, and scream out the window, "What in the name of sloppy fucks was *that*, Jerry?! From *that* lane?! Fuck!" So all cars will come with all the standard options and goodies—air con, stereo, Wi-Fi, heated seats, cruise control, mind control (wait, wha?), but now they must also have one of those tubular triangles on their roofs. Moreover, when people go to get their driver's licenses, they will be given the placard with their name and face on it to be easily slid into place for any journey. This way, if someone borrows your car, they can put *their* placard in the triangle so the blame will go to them and not you. You don't have to tell *me*. I know it's genius . . . or devious—sometimes I can't tell the distinction.

New Law Number Four: from now on there are height and width restrictions on trucks.

Yeah, you fucking heard me right. This shouldn't even be an issue, and yet every time I'm in my car some limp-dick shit head in a monstrous F-150 with jacked-up wheels almost runs me into oncoming traffic because he doesn't know (1) how big his stupid truck is, (2) how to drive his stupid truck, and (3) how to park his stupid truck, making him trawl around corners, veering into the other lanes, and almost running over pedestrians, themselves too stupid to pick up their fucking pace because "they have the right of way." Let me tell you something: "pedestrian right of way" is a great way to get your ass run over. Get the fuckin' lead out, St. Snailpace. Anyway, here's the rule of thumb: if you need a *ladder*—not a boost or a jump, but a fucking LADDER—to get in your truck, it's too big to drive in town. Take it to the fields or haul logs out of a fucking river. If you need to stop to catch your breath while you're walking around your truck, it's too big. Take it to the fields. If you're in the other lane trying to turn and you block out not only the other traffic but also any buildings or skyscrapers that were in view until you pulled up, it's too big. Take it to the fields. If you want to drive a big-ass truck, get a license to drive a semi and haul cargo like a real man would. Then at least you can do speed and drive all night.

Here's the last one. And I'm sorry, but it's brutal.

New Law Number Five: from now on the punishment is going to match the crime.

I mean, let's face it: besides jail time, what's the most severe consequences you can expect from traffic violations? Having your license revoked is *not* a deterrent. Honestly, I can't think of anyone whom that type of punishment has stopped from driving and subsequently reoffending. I know for a fact that this doesn't work. I knew a man who had so many DUIs that they took away his license. This didn't stop him from driving; in fact, he drove drunk more often because he didn't seem to give a shit. They couldn't take his license away *again*, so what were they going to do to him? What was the worst that could happen?

One night he drove home from the bar so wasted he had no idea what he was doing . . . so much so that he didn't realize he had run down a kid on a ten-speed bike until the cops showed up at his house the next morning. All the police had to do to find him was follow the carnage he'd left in his wake—smashed cars, destroyed mailboxes and blood trails—right back to his front door. He has now been in prison over ten years, and—I got to be honest—I hope he never gets out. This is what I mean when I say that losing your license, speeding tickets, and putting "boots" on cars are examples of why no one is discouraged from doing the things they continue to do. So sit down, shut up, and listen real close: if I ever take control, this is what you need to fear.

In my system, if you get in too deep with the infractions, we're taking your car, crushing it down to the size of a teacup, and giving you back a keychain. No more warnings and no more second, third, fourth, fifth, and sixth chances. You'll also never be able to buy a car in your own name again. Your name and face goes in a database designed specifically for moving violators that all car dealers and rental centers have access to; when you try to get your hands on another car, you're denied and a call goes out to the authorities. If you're caught trying to get another car, you get a very stiff fine. But here's the kicker: if we catch you behind the wheel of a car—stolen or borrowed, it doesn't matter—it's simple: WE TAKE YOUR RIGHT LEG.

Not the whole leg, mind you—just from the knee down. Fuck prison, fuck revocation . . . we take a limb. You think that's a steep price? A lot of families who've lost children or loved ones to drunk drivers, speeders, and texters might disagree with you. Now, some of you might be saying to yourself, "People who've lost legs can still drive," or, "I'll just learn to drive with my left leg." That's all well and good and your gusto can't go unappreciated. But you misunderstand. If you get caught again, WE KEEP TAKING THINGS AWAY FROM YOU. Next time you're caught we'll take the other leg. If you get caught again, we'll take an eye. If all of that doesn't drive home the hard facts of the situation, we'll take your thumbs and pinkies.

I'm not trying to sound insensitive to people with handicaps, especially those who've come home from serving their country with war wounds and deeper scars than anyone can understand. I apologize if you feel this way, and I hope this explanation will show the differentials behind my reasoning. The people I'm talking about are not dealing with an outside adversity. They chose this path to their own detriment. Soldiers coming back to the world with these sorts of injuries—duty or not—were afflicted because they were bigger on the inside than the people I'm describing in this book. Soldiers deal with a trauma that most cannot imagine, and the majority of them rise above the din to live with what has happened, leaning on each other and learning to carry on. Also, I hope people who are born with disabilities can appreciate the distinction. These people have lived their whole lives dealing with it, finding an inner strength that, in my estimation, sets them above most of the human herd. The people I'm talking about have *none* of that.

The ones who would suffer the most at the hands of these punishments don't have that kind of indomitable spirit. They don't care. If they did, they wouldn't act the way they do, and they certainly wouldn't look at anything I've said as something to learn from. They only care when it affects *them*, and that is exactly why I propose a severe admonishment for these people. They don't have the kind of spirit to rise above this kind of impairment. They don't have the kind of resourcefulness to build around something like having no legs, one eye, and six fingers left. If they did, they would have taken a cab home and come back when they sobered up. If they did, they wouldn't have

put others in danger and themselves in this particular predic-
ament. It's simply because they don't care. None of the people
in this chapter, as it pertains to driving, care about anyone but
themselves, because traffic, when all is said and done, is about
teamwork. When drivers are working together, you don't get a
lot of traffic jams. When they are not, it's like being in a fucking
video game. It's like trying to get the highest score on the worst
two hours of your life. The saddest thing is that you don't get to
put your initials on the board if and when you actually make it
to your destination.

Yeah, shit got really dark for a bit. But you forget with whom
you're talking here. I am The Great Big Mouth. I am the Infant
Finite, the beginning and the end. Sure, I'm also known as the
Boogie Knight, Captain Fluffy Bug, and the Ginger Ninja. In at
least one city in these United States I might be recognized as
Philip McCrevice or Amanda Dancewith. But never mind all
that. Don't think for a second I'm going to write a book that
doesn't try to make you laugh, cry, giggle, piss, and, most importantly, think. This is what I do. Even if the only thing this book
makes you think is, "This guy is a massive tool shed . . . " I was
successful. The worst thing you can do is leave people feeling
vapid and unresponsive. Hopefully, in my head, this book might
be the literary equivalent of a nine-volt battery to a pair of wet
balls or nipples.

Kids, don't try that at home—it does leave a mark.

I suppose I should start to merge left so I can wrap this chapter up and get off at the exit. Really, what else is there to say? My
fellow "drivers" make my life a living hell. You people make me
feel like I'm constantly cruising through some LARP-style version of *Grand Theft Auto* with *none* of the fun or benefits. You
seem worse and worse the bigger the city gets, but it's spreading

regardless. This is not a good thing; in fact, I'm convinced that all that would be required to turn things around is a global movement to pull all your fucking heads out of all your big, fat asses. I realize this is a massive wish, one that can't be resolved with one blow of the birthday candles. Also, if I thought there were a chance in hell of people turning it around on their own, I wouldn't have this chapter in the book. I wouldn't have this *book*, just a bunch of pictures of me high fiving people all over the world, stoked that we all have some good gray matter upstairs. Guess what? You're *never* going to see *that* book.

Driving is a freedom we should never take for granted. I have had so many liberating and wonderful afternoons and evenings in whatever car I've had, covering the miles with the radio on, sunglasses up, and visor down, watching America slide underneath my tires. But I have never let my attention get too far away from the fact that I am actually in control of a very big machine, one that's capable of taking lives or tasting blood. Shit can get very real behind the wheel if you aren't in the zone—school or speed or otherwise. Look, don't get the wrong idea: I don't want everyone to stop driving. I just want the dumb fucks on the road to never be allowed on the road again. That's simple enough, right? But there's that goddamn "freedom" thing I have to take into account. It's a pile of shit, if you ask me. However, I will defend to the death our right to our rights. So you can see my philosophical pickle here.

This is a very complicated problem that has one very simple solution: PAY THE Fuck ATTENTION. That's it—end of the line and end of the list. Look where the fuck you're going. Know what you're doing when you take control of the vehicle. I don't think that is too much of a stretch when it comes to requests. If you can't do that, then you shouldn't be able to hold a set of car keys, let alone guide a big-ass car around corners and byways. I just want you to fucking *think*. Your fucking smartphones aren't smart enough to think for you. They're only really smartphones if the person using them has an intelligence level slightly above "kumquat" on the human periodical table. So if you can't figure out your phone, there's no way in Gnome, Alaska, you're going to be able to figure out how to drive a damn car correctly. Selfies on phones aren't exactly simple, but they're not deadly. Selfies in cars are when you "accidentally" smash your Hyundai into a telephone pole because you were texting and driving like a fuck-ball. Knock it off.

I suffer from an almost debilitating form of road rage because I am hyper-aware and totally in tune with what's going on around me. This might be because I'm a psycho control freak who needs people to do what he wants at all times (because *that's* been going so well for me so far). But it might also be because people aren't doing what they're supposed to be doing, which is driving. You're in a car: DRIVE IT. You're in a truck: DRIVE IT. You're on a bus: you probably lost your license because you didn't DRIVE IT. I'm not an asshole; it just makes me angry when I'm always right and no one else is. When I see some cunt smearing her Maybelline on while she's driving with her knees instead of pulling over like a responsible human being (or doing her makeup before she leaves her fucking house), I want to sideswipe her car so hard she goes plummeting over a mountain somewhere. When I watch a giant cock in his giant Dodge driving around like he's King Prick of Pussy Hill, not aware that he almost ran over children and dogs for the past twelve miles, I want to get a rope, climb to the top of his truck cab, and piss in his eye sockets for being a colossal cum stain, undeserving of a license or the paycheck it takes to keep that monster filled with gas.

Only a handful of things on this planet make me angrier than shitty drivers, but it's most likely the most innocuous of anything on that list. The other stuff is pretty serious shit: bullying, child abuse, murder, racism, and so forth. So bad driving is definitely at the bottom of the maniacal food chain for me. But it's still on the chain. It's still on the hook. It pisses me the fuck off. And—wait for it . . . —it's making me hate you all. I don't like that feeling—I don't really want to hate anybody. Sure, there are people I'm always going to hate, but *everybody*? Even this Ginger Ninja likes having friends. So I guess I'm just asking everyone to be better drivers so I can have more friends. If that makes any sense to anyone, maybe you need more help than I do—at least I *know* I'm a fucking head case. But I'm the one with a book deal.

So it's this simple: if you see me in my car, remind yourself that I am armed with a loaded vehicle. As soon as you see my eyes swing your way, pull up your mental checklist. Examine your speed and be aware of the cars and trucks around you. Get off of your phone and stop eating or anything else that could distract from your ability to manage your driving experience. Take care to realize that some cars out there have precious cargo like children or PS4s. Say to yourselves, "Maybe I should get my head in the game a little stronger—I would hate for that carload of children to not get home safely, making them unable to play on those precious PS4s." The best remedy to help you avoid collisions and accidents is cognizance. Basically speaking, if you want to keep your car from getting banged up anymore than it already is, keep your eyes on the road. Keep your focus on the flow of traffic. If you need to be somewhere at a certain time, make sure you've given yourself some leeway to get there accordingly, taking into account travel length and rush-hour clogs. I'm not saying you shouldn't enjoy your drive; what I am saying is that other drivers are trying to enjoy their drives as well. Do *not* make it someone else's responsibility to pay attention for *you*. It's *your* car—do the driving.

Oh, and one more fucking thing . . .

USE YOUR FuckING TURN SIGNAL.

CHAPTER 6

MONEY—WELL . . . SPENT

I have it on good authority that a very well-known rock star, one of those icons people either figure out or flock to unnecessarily, has a rather disturbing addiction. It's a monkey that will break the back of any blue blood if allowed to flourish, but the thing is you can totally tell when the excess itself is excessive because it becomes apparent on the face and body. Yes, friends and enemies, this rock god's horrible secret is a Taco Bell habit, one that sings to the tune of more than $35 . . . A NIGHT. That's the cost just for personal use. Thirty-five bucks? Jesus skates, that's insane! The saddest piece to this resistance is it *does* show. There's no hiding a fast-food propensity, no matter how big the T-shirts get or the circumference of the waistband on your stretchy jeans. As much as I'd like to divulge who it is, I shouldn't throw stones because my own consumption of grease and bacon hasn't gone unnoticed over the years. So I'll just say to my peer, "Yo . . . easy on the Good to Go, buzz."

But, what a shock—this is a problem all over the world. Anyone who thinks this is a purely American affliction doesn't get out much. Human beings might just be the biggest they've ever been in history. Oh, by the way: not everyone can claim to be "big-boned." If you're all so big-boned, why is all that weight putting so much strain on the ligaments and tendons? If your bones were big, you'd assume that all your insides were big too. No one should feasibly be able to ride one of those rascals if they were "big-boned." I don't know how you can afford one of those scooters in the first place when your daily food budget is hundreds of dollars . . . just so you can feel "full."

Sorry, I'm miles off course here.

It's not the food I want to talk about—it's the money. Funny how a world that has been in the fluctuating grips of either depression or recession can still find the funds to waste on needless bullshit. From Oreos stuffed with cookie dough to shoes with wheels in the heels, we will find a way to make something pointless a thing of absolute value. I thought our propensity for ingenuity was gone, but I was wrong. We just took that creative imagination and applied it to the frivolous and then made sure we attached a hefty price tag to the fucker. I don't know whether it's a necessary distraction from the real issues of the world. I don't know whether it's because we're all so numb that we only feel innovative when it comes to the trivial. But I will tell you this: the balance is out of whack in a major way. The cats are out of the designer bag, and if you want them, you have to pay.

I have to hand it to the American business culture: you have got this country full of tool bags sorted out. How else can you explain the success of such *much-needed* accessories as the Buffalo Nickel Collection from the Franklin Mint? I can understand the Snuggie, but this shit is ridiculous. Better or worse still are the plate collections—I don't know whether they still sell them, but they did when I was a kid, so if it was good enough then, I have to assume they still do. It's kind of a glorious thought, really: when the world is dead and we're all gone, visitors from other planets will come here, sift through the wreckage, and find strange dishware covered in what they will misunderstand as our leaders: Scarlett O'Hara and Captain James T. Kirk.

We pay hundreds of dollars for clothes that have already been worn to shreds. We throw thousands more at lotteries the world over trying to guess those lucky five numbers and the Power-ball, just so we can *say* we're going to keep our regular jobs, but we never do. Worst of all, we blow millions on whatever we're convinced is the Next Big Thing: Furbies, Cabbage Patch Kids, juicers, Thighmasters, Atkins diets, clothes that go out of style and tech that goes out of date . . . cheap knock-offs at high-end costs, and that's just the tip of the price-berg. We chase trends like dogs and frat boys chase tails. We pitch whole paychecks into the abyss of "Gotta Fuckin' Have It," without even so much as a second glance because that's our nature. You can get mad at me all you want—shit is shit, and paint is paint. All I can do is offer the evidence. This is what we *do*. Animals are slaves to their *needs*; humans are slaves to their *wants*.

Chocolate diamonds: they're not chocolate and nobody likes them.

Stupid . . .

Think back to fifteen years ago. Smartphones weren't even a twitch in the zeitgeist's Levis in 1999. If you wanted to call home, you had to use a pay phone or use a phone at someone's house. So people like me spent a bunch of cash on prepaid phone cards and garbage like "1–800-COLLECT." Cell phones were still in their trials; they'd evolved from the monstrous models of the eighties, sure, but they were still primitive. They were either bricks with pip-pip antennae or Nextels that made your stereo crackle like there was a nuclear bomb hidden in the house, so much so that you knew when a call was coming in thirty seconds before the fucker rang. Nobody knew what a text message was, and if you wanted to surf the net, you needed a big computer. Tablets were something out of science fiction. Hell, even laptops were fairly early in the going at this point.

Then *The Matrix* happened, and everybody had to have one of those switchblade-like phones that Neo used. Hundreds of dollars later, the flip phone got better, and we had to have *that*. Another shit ton of cash later, and we had to have the Blackberry. Then the first of the iPhones hit the market and it was GAME FuckING OVER. Today any smartphone is just a different version of the iPhone. And being a sort of psycho Nostradamus, I can predict that some sort of device is going to come along and make the iPhone look like a toaster oven that only makes toast. Hey, I'm just as guilty of being a greedy fucker when it comes to blowing some coin on the latest and greatest dick teasers. But do we *need* it? And how much money are we prepared to *spend* on it?

We are a species stuck in a perpetual cycle of keeping up with the Joneses. We don't go next door to visit the neighbors anymore—we go to get a load of what they have a load of, honestly. It's the global addiction, exhibit A for why, as long as people have a choice, Communism will never last. As long as there are TVs and commercials, you're going to have the Great Craving. You threw out your VCRs for DVD players. You threw *those* out for Blu-rays. Ultraviolets gave it a go before they were slaughtered by smart TVs. All along that country road the bodies piled up: Betamax, laser discs, mini-discs, HD DVDs, and every kind of fucking gaming console you can think of. That's just *one* example of what this virus makes us do. It's incredible.

Then there's the hilarious bit in the middle here: the trash we spend our money on that, quite frankly, we would have gotten better value if we'd bent over and used the cash to wipe our asses, things like the urban parachute. In all my years of being judged for judging beings, I have yet to find something that was shilled so flagrantly, especially in the wake of the events that brought it to my attention. It wasn't bad enough that my country was shaken to its core at the time; the weasels came out of the woodwork to make a buck off the crestfallen, like the cart bearers who charged money for collecting the dead during the plague. That at least had some practicality. You'll find very little of that here.

After 9/11 I was sitting in my old apartment, watching the aftermath of the tragedy with numbed incredulity. I was worried about what was going to happen next. I was concerned about some of my friends who had been traveling that day—some of whom ended up stuck in Canada for weeks in Salvation Army camps and had no way of getting word to us. I was devastated for my country and full of rage for the people who'd attacked us. The only positive by-product was that it was bringing us all together. We were galvanized in a way that hadn't really happened since World War II. We were getting back on the horse and preparing to retaliate, and even though some of the ways we were to do so I didn't agree with, I was at least consoled by the fact that we weren't going to let this defeat us.

Then the commercials started appearing.

At first it was just gross pigs trying to capitalize on the state of the nation and its wounded patriotism: "freedom coins" and "flag packs" and "September 11 Commemorative Plates." It seemed like anyone who had a license to sell symbols of America were getting into action to fleece the demoralized masses. It was disgusting in my eyes, but I tried to ignore it; after all, I was preparing to go out on *The Pledge of Allegiance* tour, and even though it had been named months before the attacks, people certainly thought we were trying to do the same—using 9/11 to promote our shows. So I tried to shirk the ill will as best I could. Just as I was getting over the rancor and telling myself it was simply the way some people dealt with adversity, I started seeing ads for the urban parachute.

It sounds exactly like what you think it is: a backpack with a crappy parachute in it. No one who has ever gone skydiving would ever use this thing. Anyone who has ever considered BASE jumping wouldn't even give it a second thought. But nipping at the toes of the terrible footage we saw on CNN and BBC News, of people falling or jumping from the burning towers, the producers of the urban parachute were pimping these things as a way to escape terrorist attacks. I was so stunned with anger that I shut the TV off. But it all came rushing back when I saw a news piece in which the sales of the urban parachute had absolutely skyrocketed. These people had used fear to get rich with a product that ostensibly might have difficulty holding schoolbooks and note pads. I was embarrassed to be a person. I was embarrassed for my country.

That's a very severe example of how the befuddled masses clean out their bank accounts. But funnier versions can be found in the kitchen. Things like the Bacon Bowl maker, the Tortilla Bowl maker, the Slap Chop, and the Stuffed Burger maker are fucking ridiculous. Yeah sure, they work just fine, and for the first week all you make are taco salads and diced pickle relish, but when that shit runs its course, they take up space in your cupboards until you stick them in the annual garage sale for a fraction of the cost you paid for them, right next to the Harlequin Romance novels and those flared corduroys you can never seem to get rid of. The heart of the matter is that as long as you can specialize, you can make a little bread off of it, especially if it's a bread maker.

QVC and the Home Shopping Network know far too well that when people get bored, they'll spend money to keep themselves occupied. Flipping through the channels, I watched QVC sell an *entire* set of swords and knives, all "for decoration purposes only" apparently, for an inordinate amount of money, and if that "buyer clicker" was any indication of reality, they were selling those sets by the *hundreds*. I never in all my years thought that I would be surfing cable and stumble upon an auction for a medieval arsenal in the middle of the afternoon. If King Arthur had Sky TV, he could've replenished his whole army with one toll-free phone call, although he might have had to wait four to six weeks for delivery because shipping is free but overnight delivery costs extra. Does *anyone* you know need a bunch of fucking swords and knives? *Huh*? Anyone? I'm sure most of the people who bought this shit were doomsday preppers because when the zombies come and you run out of ammo, a sword will take a fucker's head right off if you swing hard enough. You won't even have to sharpen it: if some creep tries to come into your bunker, "Merlin" the stainless-steel broad sword will make sure they leave without a hand.

Oh, I'm on a madness bender today. Critical mass doesn't begin to cover where my fucking head is right now. Could it be the twelve cups of coffee? Well, technically, I usually put two K-Cups in each mug, so I'm pushing *twenty-four* at the moment— appropriate because I'm starting to feel like Jack Bauer in the grips of a season finale. I'm unhinged and unfettered: no time for dalliances, Dr. Jones. Seriously, all jokes aside, I might look into having myself declassified from being "human" because it's getting embarrassing. I can't allow myself to be lumped in with a genus or species that commits these many acts of idiocy—I've got a rep to protect . . . sure, it's pretty soiled itself, but hey! I'm trying, goddamnit!

As I've said earlier in the book, I run on the boardwalk in Venice, California, a lot. I see a lot of shit that's fairly endearing, like families coming down to the beach to see the ocean and older couples walking the bike paths together to stay fit. I know, right? I say "Awwww . . . " too! It's fucking adorable—the older couples even wear matching outfits. I love seeing that. It gives me hope that maybe love is essential to our longevity as a whole. Then again, when you hear what I'm about to describe, the key to survival may just become keeping key funding away from dildos who can't be bothered to do anything productive except suck air and shit. I'm getting away from my point; let me do my best to stay on target here for a second.

When I run on the beach, I see a lot of different people down there: other joggers, families walking their dogs or pushing their babies in carriages, friends heading down to Muscle Beach to pump up in public, and so forth. I also have to dodge a lot of people renting giant bicycles nicknamed "beach cruisers"— big ol' monsters that look like throwbacks from the 1950s. Just watching these people ride the fuckers, I can tell it takes some real quad and leg strength to keep them upright, let alone rolling on the concrete. I can't help but wonder, however, why they don't just walk and check shit out—the path runs right by the Santa Monica Pier, and it takes two seconds to turn and run up the steps, down the boards, and to the sea. But regardless of what I think of these beach cruisers, at *least* they're getting some exercise. They're exerting energy and burning some calories off their fat asses.

It's the people on the Segways that give me fucking gas.

There are whole gangs of people going on little tourist-y tours of the boardwalk who just can't fathom the thought of actually *walking* on their own. So there are services that take people on guided tours (I don't know why they're "guided"—you can see the fucking ocean from four blocks away), and they're all riding Segways. They spent money on a trip, they paid good coin for hotel rooms, rental cars, and various souvenirs and such . . . and then they go and blow their cash renting a motorized walker. A Segway is nothing more than a podium on wheels. Here's the real kicker: NO ONE LOOKS COOL ON A SEGWAY. I don't give a rat's cherry kiss who you are; Brad Pitt, straight from the set of *Fight Club* looking fit as fuck and ready to strike, would look like an asshole on a Segway. It's even worse when they're all wearing helmets. Yes, I know the creator of the Segway accidentally drove himself off a cliff, but these fuckers are literally at sea level, surrounded by sand on one side. You still look like a dick, and you should feel like a dick for spending money on it.

I wonder if anyone told them, "Hey, man . . . you know walking is *free*, right?"

They cruise by on their rented Segways, taking up more of the path than they should, smiling and pointing and not paying *any* attention to what the fuck they're doing. I saw a whole gang of them dressed in their out-of-town camouflage (pastels and shorts above the knee), and they nearly ran *over* a woman pushing her toddler in a baby stroller. Then they didn't even stop to check whether she was okay because they didn't know it had happened—that's how oblivious they were. They just kept smiling and pointing like an incompetent army trying to invade Easter Island on a chocolate egg hunt. Bigger pricks might exist, but as they go, in my parlance, I have yet to dodge them on a wave of rolling contraptions.

The shit is everywhere: Kobe beef costs hundreds of dollars, people pay thousands to eat flakes of gold with their food, and if you've got the millions to back it up, you can even eat an endangered animal if you know the right restaurants. High fashion is a player's market: spread a rumor that a burlap sack is "tres bon," and you'll see racks of them on Beverly Drive. It's like the world can't wait to waste money on something people *say* is worth it. All the conspiracy nuts in America are convinced that there is no gold backing up our currency, but none of them can take a second to swing their cantankerous, stubborn observations at what we're spending our "worthless" money on in the interim. Knowing a few of these maniacs personally, I can tell that if they ever did get involved, it would be an Internet sensation: Gucci bags on the grassy knoll, shark meat being sold in the Beverly Hills Hotel kitchen, and pricy, irritatingly sarcastic T-shirts floating on the waters of the Bermuda Triangle.

This is an issue I've been keeping track of for quite some time. I remember when I was a kid, every heavy-metal kid who rode a skateboard wanted a Metallica "Pushead" deck. And I do mean *everyone*. We'd talk about them before school when we'd smoke cigarettes in the parking lot. We'd discuss them at lunch when we smoked behind the gym. We'd dream about them as we rode home on our cheap knock-off boards . . . while we smoked, yes. I've been smoking a long time. Quit focusing on that for a second and get back on this side of the fence. Are you there? No? Jesus fucking bastard Christ, FINE! I'll quit fucking smoking! Yes, I *know* it's relevant to this chapter because I waste money on cartons of the damn things! We'll talk about that *later*! Okay? Man . . . hold on, let me catch my breath . . .

Anyway, so my friends and I all coveted the Metallica Pushead board, or the "Zorlac" deck, as they are sometimes called. The problem is that they were expensive, at least as far as we were concerned. We all came from middle-income families or worse, so the amount of money these boards cost were like, "We might as well buy a car!" This, however, did nothing to stop us from wishing we had one: riding around like a king in a crown, holding onto bumpers like Marty McFly, and swooping by the kids gathered in front of Bunger Intermediate. Before you start on the "Bunger" jokes, let me get to the gist of this exploratory little tale. Finally one of our compatriots achieved glory for the ages: for his birthday he was given our holiest of grails: a brand-new Zorlac board, complete with fresh trucks and Slime Ball wheels. It was a thing to appreciate—killer Pushead design underneath and plenty of grip tape for the bottom of his duct-taped Converse shoes.

We were all on hand for the unveiling and subsequent first skate. My friend, who I'll call Jon, grinned from ear to ear. "It's so bad ass, right?" he exclaimed, holding it above his head. We were all too absorbed in its shininess to pay attention to him—seventh graders aren't really known for their discipline. But we all dutifully stood back for the inaugural ride. Jon put it on the ground and placed one foot on it, scanning around to drink in our obvious envy and smiling like someone was going to take his picture. "Check it out!" he said, and pushed off, swinging it around at the end of his street and flooring it back toward us with pure relish. With a nice kick flip, he brought it back to his hand and held it up again. "Dude, this thing is so rad!" With that, Jon jumped in the air for an acid drop.

When he landed, the board snapped in half.

We would find out later that this was a problem that turned out to be quite prevalent with the early renditions of the

Metallica board. It wasn't the band's fault, but it was true. They almost all split in half. They were made of what looked like particleboard or plywood. Sure, they looked "The Shit," but they were good for maybe one trick and then broke like waves on the shore. It's difficult to correctly explain the heaviness that hung in the air as Jon stood there stunned, looking at his "bitchin' board" that was now broken and unusable. The silence sat like a fart in a sauna, dank and foul. Then a crushing scream came from Jon that I have rarely heard elsewhere in my life. "WHAT THE Fuck, DUDE?" he spat as the reality sank back to our hemisphere. "YOU HAVE GOT TO BE FuckING KIDDING! MY PARENTS ARE GONNA FuckING MURDER ME!" We all came closer to see the remnants of what was, at one time, the object of all our desires. If I'm remembering this right, Jon picked the two halves of the board up gingerly and sulked back to his home, dejected and ruined, knowing the hell he was in for when he reached his destination. I also think that in that moment I realized that expense doesn't always guarantee quality. You can spend a lot of money on something, but that might not get you anything worth a shit in the end. I may have had some slips over the years, but overall that is a lesson I am determined not to forget.

We all have a habit of developing spending frenzy. Look at all the people who went out and spent hundreds on those special shoes that were supposed to tone your butt: you know, the ones that made every woman wearing them look like they all had clubbed feet. After millions of dollars spent around the world, it turned out those same shoes created more back and knee problems than they really let on. Oh, and Tamagotchis—you remember those? They were digital pets on key chains that everyone and their mom *had* to have! A bunch of pointless capital hurled in their direction later, they now reside in either the basements of the world or the eternal baskets reserved for annual spring sales. Isn't it silly what we choose to splurge on in the heat of the golden moment? Isn't it sad how we never learn from those lessons as the cycle repeats itself over . . . and over . . . and over?

I can go back even further: old ladies dying in pursuit of those Cabbage Patch Kids, the Rubik's Cube, the Wacky Wall Crawler, the Sega Dreamcast, that copy of Madonna's first book, those JNCO pants with all the fucking zippers, the Thighmaster, the Ab Belt, the Shake Weight, the SodaStream, the . . . you know what, this is getting ridiculous. If I kept going, there'd be no more room left in this book for the rest of my curses, blue humor, and quirky observations. Let me just sum it up by saying this: none of you can be trusted with the freedom of free trade. I know right now you're thinking to yourself, "This coming from the man who spent $10,000 at a fucking Best Buy?" Yes indeed, this guy right here, with the Vault full of movies to show for it, is saying to you the time has come for the human race to run their monetary ideas by me for the rest of their lives. Yeah, I don't like it any more than you may, but shit has happened on my side of the yard. Lap it up, fuzz balls.

We live in a world where people can't stay in their houses, let alone pay their bills. Kids are *starving*—not hungry, STARVING— and big business has a stranglehold on the planet like never before. Yet most of the world strolls past like it's nothing. They cross their streets and hope to die while the others stick needles in their own eyes so as not to see the disparate levels of suffering that they have no control over. The rich are *really* rich and the poor are *holy shit* poor, and the bit in the middle where we all would feel comfortable is getting smaller and smaller to the point at which we can't slip paper in between them. When the world can't take care of its own, when the chips are stacked against the spread, something has got to fucking give. So here's my solution, because I always seem to have one: every time you buy something pathetically insipid, you have to donate the equivalent amount of money to a charity that fights for the poor.

That's the long and lean of it. I will cease firing off on the masses for wiping their asses with money that could be used elsewhere if they keep the status quo in line by helping other people who desperately need it. Outrageous, you say? I beg to differ. You see, most of the people who fall under the poverty level are just folks who *want* to work, but many American businesses still farm out good jobs overseas, and this is a problem all over the world. These people are descendants of the salty fuckers who helped build and defend this world, no matter where you happen to live. When that spirit is being crushed because the bottom line is self-serving, then something drastic has to be done. Maybe, *just* maybe, if I'm the motherfucker who has to sign off on the checks and balances, people will stop throwing away good money on bad decisions. If they continue to spend but give the equal amount to the people who need it, we all win. Maybe people will spend less but on more essential things, while they also give back to the people who need help. The grip of Big Business will slacken when we start to put our best feet forward. We will no longer be hostages of The Man, the poor will get a chance to get back on their feet, and The Man will have no power over us anymore. Good night and good luck, Big Brother: it's time to stick up for each other now.

In the end we're all just exceptional monkeys with credit limits—Simian Grundy, born on a Monday, flush on Tuesday, and broke on Hump Day. On a good day we commit ourselves to the myth of the fiscal loaves and thrifty fishes, wiling away our bank accounts on any whim without a thought of the long term or the consequences. It is damn near pornographic; the gross distinction between the Haves and the Have-Nothings is so out of whack, you couldn't slide a bike tire in the space that separates them. This wouldn't bother me if the world at large weren't so bent on impressing itself with shallow baubles and temporary distractions. Am I the only asshole who feels like our analog souls are in digital jeopardy? Buzz-kill alert: I guess I am the last one to get asked for the dance. But I stand by my record, even if it's a 78 playing at 33⅓.

Any kids who don't understand that parable, I give you permission to ask your parents to explain. Just don't show them the chapter about "The Head Song," which you haven't read because I haven't written it yet, so forget I suggested it—ABORT! ABORT MISSION!

Let me tell you a silly little story about how I almost blew myself up.

In 2000 I was in the whirlwind called the Slipknot Touring Machine. We had been on the road nonstop since Ozzfest '99, jumping from tour to tour and exacting vengeance on the music scene that had refused to go where we wanted it to go. Thus, when I'd first started touring, I moved some of my stuff into my Gram's house to keep my bills low (also because they turned our old apartment into a bed and breakfast, but that's neither here nor there). But I'd sold my car as well, so when I *was* at home, I had nothing to drive. As a result, when I had a rare week off to myself, I decided I was going to buy a new car— better yet, a truck, with big, old-school wheel wells and the smell of a decade I wasn't born in! I wasn't exactly rolling in dough, so I went down to a used car lot to take a gander at what my options could be in that area. Luckily there was one not too far from my grandmother's house. I sauntered over to check out the selection.

I was in luck—there was indeed a truck that met my criteria right there in the lot! It was rusty and ragged out, but I loved it. I could hardly wait to give it a test drive. I took it out for a spin around the corner and liked what I was feeling, so I pulled back in, put cash down (maybe a little more than I felt it was worth, but I really liked that truck), and drove away, humming along to the only AM station I could tune in on the radio. The handling was shit, the exhaust leaked into the cab, the whole truck reeked of gasoline, and the tires felt washy, but I didn't let that get me down. In retrospect, maybe I should have let it get me a *little* down.

I got it back to my place and hung out with some friends for a while. I was hungry by the time they left, so I grabbed my keys to go procure the finest of fast foods. I jumped in the truck, stuck the key in, gave it a turn . . . and it wouldn't start. I'd just bought the thing and it wouldn't start. I gave it a jump-start with my Gram's car, went to Hardee's, slammed a burger, and went home. After I'd shut off the engine, I had a funny feeling it wasn't going to start again. So I tried the ignition; once again it didn't start. As I was just about to use my Gram's car to bring the bastard back to life again, I noticed the long trail of liquid that seemed to stretch from my driveway and all the way down the street. Upon inspection I realized with dread that the fucking truck had been leaking gas since I'd bought the son of a bitch. It also occurred to me that as I was examining the spilt gas, I had a lit cigarette sticking out of my mouth. Good one, Taylor. Maybe next time you could set yourself on fire before you surround yourself with flammable fluids.

The fucked-up thing is that when I took the truck back to trade it in, the guy I bought it from tried to blame me for the fact that the truck was a grade-A piece o' shit. I'd had the thing for a total of three hours, but he was convinced that in that space of time I'd blown the engine and spiked the gas tank. Before I told him he was an idiot—and prior to a certain urge to punch the dick munch in his dumb ass face—I reminded him with an incredible amount of restraint that I had buyer's insurance and that legally he had to give me another car for the same value if anything came up in the first twenty-four hours of ownership. Begrudgingly he offered me the only other car on the lot that seemed like it was worth a shit: a white Berlinetta with a black "bra" on the hood and a fairly orange interior. With a resigned sigh and a grip on the keys, I took it for a test drive, pulled into a parking lot, shut it off, started it over again, and, after deciding it would do, I traded that truck for that car, clean across and no harm done.

Now, you may be saying to yourself, "Self, how does that work? Why on God's green cricket pitch would he go back to the *same* dealership and get another car, after the first one was a trash heap, instead of just getting his money back and going somewhere else?" That is indeed a wonderful question: Why would I bother with another selection from a used car dealer that clearly didn't give a rat's scratch about the state of the automobiles they sold? The answer is simple: I was so stressed out about the experience that I didn't want to deal with it anymore, so I just accepted my lot with a modicum of ignorant grace and got the fuck out of there. I just wanted a car that would run and be done with it. So I was left with a car I didn't really want at a price I was positive was about three times too much for it. But here's the kicker: a week later I put a car stereo in it that was worth more than the car. Four months later, as that car sat in my Gram's driveway, it was broken into and the thieving pricks stole the stereo. They also took all of my CDs, but that was more my fault than anybody else's—I shouldn't have left them in the car in the first place. Long story short, I was a knob of the highest caliber. I'd wasted all that money on a car that wasn't even cool when it first came out, and then I lost a stereo that was better than the car itself. If they'd taken the car and left the stereo, I would've high-fived them and appreciated their efforts. But alas, this was not to be. When I eventually sold the Berlinetta, I lost about two grand on the deal, but good riddance. I just wanted it out of my life. It was just a constant reminder of how fucking stupid I could be with my money.

Let me close this chapter out by saying I accept that what you buggers do with your money is honestly none of my business. I know that all too well. Sometimes when I'm with acquaintances and they're on the verge of a horrible fiscal decision, I keep my trap shut. You know why? How else are they going to learn? If they want to dig up and construct that giant ball pit in their backyard when their children are on the verge of being too old to enjoy it, who am I to say anything? If some of them want to get their old Honda Accord detailed and painted so it looks like a gilded turd on the highway, what am I going to say to stop them that wouldn't leave me looking like a hypocritical jackass? I mean, fuck, I very nearly blew my own face off with a lit cigarette because I bought a truck that should have been taken out into a field and shot long ago. I am no authority on what represents a good purchase and a bad buy.

However, class . . . write this down:

Dumb is dumb.

It's that simple. But there's dumb and then there's bloody embarrassing, and what some of you are up to with your fair-earned expenses can plainly be regarded as embarrassing. The consternation with which you scramble and pursue each "precious" expenditure is very nearly fascinating if it weren't so very aggravating. You *could* for a hobby just chuck your dollars, pounds, yen, loonies, rubles, and Euros directly into a burn barrel and set it ablaze. It might just warm your soul as well as your hands, and they'd at least be put to better use considering what you *do* do (heheh . . . doodoo . . .) with these funds. Between the rainbow-colored toe socks and the gun-metal-gray Hummers, insanity reigns supreme at the checkout counters of Earth, and this at a time when charity is a dirty word and kindness describes good weed more than good deeds. Don't even get me started on the extreme coupon crazies: buying toilet paper in bulk to save pennies on the dollar makes sense until you get a yeast infection. Then you're stuck with fluffy fanny ribbon that gives you runny bits for a year and no real way of unloading it on someone else. Fucking weird . . .

This need, this fire for extra and more might just leave us all scarred and covered in soot, and for what? A house loaded with trends and piddly shit that may not carry the same value in years to come? How fair is that to all those hours you put in working your ass off? Can we be okay with the spirits that make us scrounge for one more nickel, one more dime in order to get those fancy towels with the queen's face on them, lording over the phrase, "I DRY THEE FOR THE EMPIRE"? What about those apps you've bought on your phones that now collect mega pixels of dust because you played them for a few months but then had to have the next hot app? Sure, you can say, "It's only a buck here and a buck there—what's the hurt?" What do you say to yourself when you realize you've got $125 worth of worthless apps on your phone, money you could've used to make a car payment or make your rent before you get behind? The point is: all of this adds up, and you ultimately pay the price.

If you're younger, you won't understand this. Money still has that "parents' coffers" feel to it when you're young. It's the magical replenishing cupboard that always has cereal, always has milk, always has juice or soda, and always has money for gas and smokes. But the older you get, the more you begin to appreciate the fact that money is finite—it's not always so readily made to go around. I could sit back and blame parents who are bound and determined to make sure their kids have it better than they did, but again I'd make myself look like a major two-faced idiot. The biggest thing I can say is that I might be overprotective when it comes to the people I take care of. Deep inside, though, I know I might be doing my kids a disservice by not teaching them early on about the value of money, and that kind of value deserves respect and responsibility. Because of this I've had to start over, training my kids about what's what and how's now. It hurts but it's vital, and in the long run it will benefit everyone.

I encourage you all to do the same. Don't be so frivolous with money you had to get your ass kicked to earn. Don't throw it at crap you can do without. If you can afford it, really take a look at what you're getting and then ask yourself, "Am I going to use this for a long time?" Get the most out of what you get. There is nothing bad about passing on a temporary distraction to save up for that permanent pastime. Some shit does go a long way. Some stuff is worth an investment. But there are a lot of pitfalls and platitudes swimming in the primordial gravy, poised to divorce you from your coin purses. If you're smart, you'll get the radar up and running before the kamikazes strafe you and your money clips are empty. Every commercial, ad, spam e-mail, and product placement on the planet is hell bent—not heaven sent—and they don't care about you. They don't care about your homes, your rent, your children or their college funds, your worries or your strife. Their bare necessities are your money, and if necessary, they will indeed strip you bare.

I don't want you to look back on some shit with regret. I want you to feel like you know what you're doing. Take a better hand in what's afoot. As much as I love to point and laugh at you, I have plenty of other shit I can use to tickle my funny bone. To quote the creepy man who purportedly owns J. G. Wentworth, "It's *your* money. Use it when you need it." Even if you want that special something, show some restraint. Because skin might come back and the forests may replenish themselves over time, but money ain't green because it's growing. If it's gone, it's gone.

Time's running out.

Act NOW!

CHAPTER 7

GET ALONG, LITTLE DOGGIES

It was a balmy, enigmatic night back in the year of our Lord one thousand nine hundred and ninety-two, at the head of an uneven driveway on the south side of Des Moines, Iowa.

A night like any other, really, it was a night when you talked to hear other people, not just because you were in love with the sound of your own voice. It was a night for iced tea and laughing . . . a Lemonade Evening, as I like to call them. It was one part reflection, one part distraction, and, most importantly, several parts ambition. The discussions held in that driveway were some of the most vigorous and emotional I've ever had the privilege to be a part of, especially when the minds and hearts involved were just as devoted as my own. Some people would crouch on the concrete stoop step, perpendicular to the front door of my Gram's house and the street fifteen away. Others might be perched on their own cars; others still took up real estate on the hood of my grandmother's brown four-door car, a model that to this day is still a mystery to me—it could have been a Chevy and it could have been a Ford; all I know is that by the time of the night in question I'd thrown up in that car twice and four of my friends had committed sexual appeasements behind it when the street lights were low enough to hide them. But I still remember the license plate number: UAK 470. Look close—it has "AK47" in the middle of it. That was my Gram's brown car of indeterminate make—a true South Side original.

My friends and I huddled on the steps there on late nights, after band practice or parties, so we could talk good shit. You never knew where the conversations would go, but you knew they would be perfect for the moment at hand. It was exquisite fat chewing, slinging slang; you could get away with murder if you phrased it just right, and if you did they'd thank you for the kill. We sat there, smoking cigarette after cigarette, drinking twenty-ounce after twenty-ounce of various sodas that were usually laced with something a little more satanic, avoiding our duties for a little while, plotting our invasion of the real world, the adult world. These were the moments filled with thoughts that were never laid to rest, only left on the low burners so they never ever cooked off too quickly. It's important for you to understand our states of being, our absolute steadiness even as our aspirations broke on the waves of excitement that seemed to keep on coming. We were originals, you see. We were one of a kind and proud of it. The world would never see us coming . . . and it never did.

Yes, this driveway was ground zero for rounds of ribbing and out-and-out brutal matches designed to make you crow like a Lost Boy or chew your lip in defeat, known to those in the know as the Dozens. It was also perfect staging for some fairly infamous speeches in our circle of beastly friends and trust: the Square Foot scenario, the Jar of Marbles soliloquy, the Night of the Fake Ninja Practice, the Temperature/Thermometer debate, the Bad Sipa Sack gathering, the "Live, Mighty Cougar!" embarrassment, the Burning High Hat experiment, and, most importantly, the Fat Suit Album Cover fantasy. On that stoop I lied to a complete stranger about a father I didn't know rather than admit I had absolutely no clue as to who, where, or what he was. On that stoop I suffered at the hands of humility—I was ashamed of myself more times than I care to admit, throwing my stubborn pride into the faces of people I claimed to care about and never *ever* admitting when I was wrong. So you see, that stoop was a place of both comedy and tragedy. But let's get back to the comedy before I bum myself out.

It was into this world of imagination and cogitation that something occurred, something so utterly ridiculous I can only tell it now in this context. It came out of nowhere, like a thunderstorm around a sand castle, so completely out of place that you felt stunned for a really long time, and it was a chore to rouse yourself from it. The ludicrous hilarity of it all is so genuine and so low-rent that to this day I smile just thinking about it. In remembrance it actually makes sense that something like this would happen. It fit with the society we were smack in the middle of: the suburbs of the south side, slack in jaw and stacked with jocks, cheerleaders, and fifties affinities. Against this backdrop I was the devil in blue jeans, the crazy kid the neighbors complained about, listening to loud heavy music of all kinds on the roof of my house and staring down the stuffed sweaters who walked by. This almost felt like a reverse prank. But the people involved didn't get the memo, and thank shit for that.

That night it was just me and Shawn Economaki sitting outside, mixing it up. I believe there were some people in the house. But it was just the two of us hanging out in the muted darkness, the fading sense of light cascading on the street leaving us in relative shadowed privacy. At that hour nobody was driving by, really, and we were laughing and talking good shit. I had my acoustic guitar in my hands and was playing chords absentmindedly as we continued to josh on our own terms. My Gram's brown car was parked right up next to the porch step; you couldn't really see us sitting there from the street. So you can imagine our reaction when a late-seventies Monte Carlo pulled up right in front of my Gram's house and parked—on the wrong side of the street, pointed in the opposite direction.

At first we just thought it was friends of ours, coming over to see what kind of mischief was on the dance card that evening. But as I peeked over the top of Gram's car I could see that this car only had two people in it—a man and a woman, neither of whom I recognized. Shawn and I were a bit perplexed for a second. Shawn even said, "What in the Fuck?" We kept vigil, wondering aloud whether they were planning something nefarious. Then, all of a sudden, our answers came out swinging, and it was an answer so obvious we felt stupid we hadn't realized it to begin with. As we watched from the shadows, the woman in the passenger seat took one last look around and then dove head-first into the man's lap. I'm no doctor, but it didn't take me long to figure out what she was doing. Once we did, however, it was everything we could do not to howl with laughter.

We sat there for a second, trying to figure out how to handle this. I certainly wasn't going near that car—any couple this "classy" was sure to have a gun stuffed somewhere. However, I didn't want two gross people sucking each other off in front of my grandmother's house. What was I going to do? Just like that, I had an epiphany. There was a modified C-chord phrasing I'd been toying around with over the last few days, played way up on the twelfth fret, that had a fairly Spanish tinge to the sound it made. There was no progression for it to go with; it was just this weird chord thing I had been fucking around with that had no real home musically for me. It hit me that night: I looked at my acoustic guitar, smiled at Shawn, and said, "Should I play the head song?"

Shawn laughed and said, "The *what*?" And before I knew what the hell I was doing, I had jumped up on the hood of Gram's brown car thing, fretting this high chord, strumming furiously, and caterwauling like Jim Carrey attempting to sing a flamenco song, akin to Chevy Chase in *The Three Amigos*. It was so loud that it scared both of us, but Shawn fell on the ground in hysterics. I could barely keep the singing going because I was choking back my own fits of laughter. The effect was instantaneous: the woman's head shot up out of the guy's crotch. The man, abruptly pulled from the ledge of sex, reacted like he'd been hit with a baseball bat during a nap. The Monte Carlo fired up and began to pull away *fast*. I jumped off the hood and ran up the street after them, still singing out of key but shaking the shit out of every note, like a tone-deaf opera singer on filibuster, refusing to relinquish the stage for anything. When I did stop, I collapsed in the grass by the curb and giggled like a kid with a secret.

It was after telling the story a couple hundred times to my friends, complete with a rendition of the Head Song, that I realized the most important part of the tale is the ridiculous couple, pulling over in the suburbs so the guy could get a blowjob and the woman could suffer through it. Over the years I've tried to create an interesting backstory for these voyeurs. Maybe they were married and it was their anniversary, this little excursion coming from the husband's request to spice things up. Maybe she was trying to score some drugs off the guy and this was the price she had to pay. Maybe they were swingers and were hoping someone who happened to pass by might join them. Either fucking way, one thing's for sure: people do dumbass fucking shit together. This is the price we pay for relationships—sexual, romantic, or otherwise.

Now, before we get into this messy text, let's outline what the word "relationship" actually entails, shall we? To do that, I'm going to go right to Dictionary.com for the definition, but fear not: there will still be running commentary (and maybe a dick joke).

re·la·tion·ship [ri-**ley**-sh*uh*n-ship] *noun*

1. a connection, association, or involvement.

Well, that's real helpful, isn't it? It's pretty damn general if you ask me. . . . People have connections, associations, and involvements with a lot of things, such as lactose, TV psychics, and clothes dryers during use if you lean in close and correctly.

2. connection between persons by blood or marriage.

Okay, that's getting a little more specific. This could mean anything from marriage to sibling rivalry. Being in a band has the feel of both, without the sexy payoffs. Well, I guess it depends on who you're in a band with . . .

3. an emotional or other connection between people: *the relationship between teachers and students.*

That can take on a whole *list* of other meanings—way to go, web. "The relationship between teachers and students" . . . that could mean anything from how much I hated my ninth-grade English teacher to the lady who went to prison because she fucked her student so many times they had kids together.

4. a sexual involvement; affair.

Bingo: the Hunka Chunka. That's what I call a relationship. I believe that's what everybody else in the world considers a relationship as well.

Relationships can be intense, like a heated romance or rivalry. They can be fairly innocuous, like the way we treat coworkers or people we go to church with—not that I would know anything about that. It can be a specific energy between yourself and a nonhuman, like food, clothes, and such. Relationships are the balance one strikes between oneself and the outside world. It's a very relative term, because everyone has a relationship with something or someone. It's like referring to something as "natural." No shit, Mr. Holmes. Thanks for the fucking head's-up.

Another relationship we all have to deal with is with our family, blood or otherwise. I have to be honest: it's getting brutal out there. Family reunions, established as a way for tight-knit broods to stay close as they grew up and moved away, have now become something of a UFC title fight with fried chicken and that shitty lime-green Jell-O that no one eats. There are whole limbs and branches of family trees that can never be spoken of in certain company. "Why aren't the Boones here this year?" "*Fuck* those people—Janice can't keep her *fucking* mouth shut!" Seriously, it's like *Game of Thrones* with a softball game at the end that no one really wants to be a part of but everybody desperately wants to win.

I have been blessed with an amazing family here in what I call the "Afternoon of My Life." My wife's family has accepted me in a way I've never felt before in all my years on this plane. So let me say, with all the love in the world . . . they are *the* biggest bunch of crazy people I have ever known in my life. From the Bonnicis to the Bennetts, every one of them is wonderful, weird, and utterly unforgettable. They are ALL LOUD. They are incredibly opinionated. They love with the strength of the Hulk on deep Gamma saturation. They scare me a little, and I love every minute I get to be with them. Don't get me wrong: I love my side of the family as well. But my family is a little more scattered, and there are only a handful I'm really close with, like my Gram and my cousins. My in-laws? They are a lot like if the Avengers and the Justice League got together for Margarita

Monday and decided to spend the whole night debating everything from quantum physics to why *Quantum Leap* should have
never been canceled.

Every dinner starts and ends the same way: screaming over
the top of each other. Here's the scene: fifteen of us all waiting
for a table at the Cheesecake Factory. Some are milling about
outside smoking cigarettes and others are inside making comments about the many and varied cheesecake flavors that have
manifested over the years. "Turtle cheesecake: why would they
have turtle cheesecake? I bet it's rich . . . " We finally get a table
outside under the heaters, and the Bataan Dinner March begins.
Some break off to go to the bathroom and thereby spend another
ten minutes trying to find the table, hoping the others ordered
the appetizers they wanted. It takes another thirty minutes to
decide what everyone wants to eat.

The whole time the conversation swings from the important—"I really think she needs to go to the doctor, that thing
looks swollen"—to the banal—"I am *not* taking down my Christmas lights! Those colors are seasonal, and I think they look better in the summer anyway!"—to the insane—"You do this *every*
time we come here. We *know* you're upset they changed your
favorite dish, Corey. Suck it up and get a damn hamburger."
Eventually the debate begins over who owes what and how to
tip and who wants the leftovers. Finally the long loud procession
moves toward the front door, where, as most of us smoke, the
good-byes take another thirty minutes to bid farewell to people
we will most likely see the very next day. This is a typical night
out for dinner: five minutes driving, ten minutes waiting, thirty
minutes eating, two hours talking about pretty much anything
that comes to mind. You may think it's a bit crazy, but I love it.

I suppose that, besides family, the one relationship we all have
in common is the herald of pain and compensation rogue CDs:

the girlfriend/boyfriend. For a lot of us this is our last taste of an uninitiated experience. I mean, let's face it: we grow up with family, we come of age developing friendships, and in between we're all just adjusting to responsibilities like education, respect, and ethics. And just when you think you've got the whole science of life on a lockdown, puberty comes and hits you in the nuts and tits and throws this wrench called sexual tension in the bitch's brew. As an adolescent—not quite young and sure as shit not old—this is like having to start from scratch because, depending on what your sexual preference turns out to be, you have to relearn who you are all over again. The end result can be awesome, but that shit ain't right.

So with that kind of adversity hanging over all our heads at such an early age, we proceed to trounce down a path of ridiculous mistakes that eventually leads to the idiocy we can all relate to, gay or straight, man or woman: the Dating Scene. Seems simple here on digital "paper": having years of experience trying and failing to attract members of the opposite or identical sex, you'd think we'd have worked the kinks out, pun intended. But as it turns out, life and karma have even more strange adventures for you to endure. Funny that: anything else we'd spent half our lives working at we might actually get better at. Actually, because we spend so much time doing it the *wrong* way, we get set in those wrong ways and develop hang-ups, aversions, and cold silences. What in the virtual fuck is *that*?

The crazy thing is that romantic relationships can lead to sex—something any sane person would *love* to do. With that in mind, you'd think we'd put more effort into figuring out the best way through the mind field. Nope. Not even close. I've got it sorted. Here's the thing: for guys, when it comes to other men or women, we almost always revert unconsciously to whatever worked the first time we got someone into bed. It doesn't matter if it was ninth grade or last week, guys have a tendency to compartmentalize the shit that works and forget what wasn't effective, thereby giving them a wheelhouse they can consult when in jeopardy. However, we as dudes forget the cardinal rule: all keys do *not* work on all doors. Men and women have different things that turn them on, and believing that one way works across the board, sexual or otherwise, is a recipe for disastrous relationships. If men can just learn to adapt to each situation until they find the one that fulfills them the most, they would be a lot happier, as would their partners, and they'd spend less time at Happy Hour or pounding the shit out of the heavy bag at the gym.

Women have a worse dilemma: they watch too many fucking movies.

Nicholas Sparks and all those others have *got* to fucking stop with the sappy, saccharine rom-com dramedy flicks that make all men on Earth look like either spineless wishy-washy ball bags or knuckle-dragging shit heels who don't give a shit about anything other than cars, beer, and pussy. Although some men certainly fit that bill, shit just ain't like that. But you women watch Ryan Gosling and Josh Duhamel and fucking think, "Why can't more men be like them?" Simple: IT IS A FuckING MOVIE. They're like that because the SCRIPT DICTATES SUCH. Not saying they're not decent chaps in real life, but Judas fucking Iscariot . . . *The Notebook? The Vow?* Are you completely fucking with me? Shit like that is possible but not plausible; real life keeps going past the happy endings and rolling credits. But regardless of the chances of things like this happening, women heap these expectations on us men, who can barely keep the "brown parentheses" out of our Hanes briefs (easy: no more white underwear). You want to talk about walking into the game with a handicap? Men have a snow cone's chance in a furnace of making a woman happy on their own merits. So most men fake it for a while but then give up because it's fucking exhausting. How many more times can we stand in the rain and tell you how we waited for you forever, praying to God that our shirt looks good across our pecks even though we didn't do that many push-ups that morning? Christ, it's like playing baseball blindfolded while you're swinging at grenades.

I'm not saying all men and women are like that; I'm saying most men and women fall into these traps. But I can also see the "disease" spreading. If there were a worldwide survey laden with honesty, I bet it would show masturbation is on the rise on both sides of the gender fences. I can't blame people: who the fuck wants that kind of pressure when it comes to something that should feel good inside and out? Look, I'm no Dr. Ruth, but I can tell the difference between smart choices and incompetent theory. The problem comes when no one talks to each other. How the fuck are we suppose to *really* know what turns someone on without actually getting to know them? None of us can be bothered. If we spent more time talking and less time texting, we'd pick up on so much more. People can't even look up from their smartphones long enough to pay attention to where they are *walking*. You expect them to have the capacity to put in the kind of effort it takes to get to know someone past name, rank, and what they order at Starbucks? Good fucking luck.

This isn't just a romantic problem. People of the planet Earth are trying to download themselves into tiny screens and fancy-looking Oakley sunglasses. They consider time spent surfing the social networking sites the same as hanging out with real live flesh-and-blood humans. Then why are we all so uncomfortable and awkward when we sit down with other humans? It's very simple: real life has no memes, no headers, no tweet history, no bios, and no portfolios of pictures to pick through at your most convenient disposal. You have to actually *talk* to people. That's how you get to know someone. Sorry that sharing space with "icky humans" isn't as sterile and clinical as you'd like it. Then again, after seeing what goes on in these "clubs," I wouldn't want to hang out with other people either. From the shit I witness on the dance floor to what some of these dudes try to do to women when they think they've had enough booze to get away with it, those seem to be the grossest places ever imagined. Even Caligula would stay home. If you go to those places, I'm telling you now: your evening is going to end with gonorrhea at best and *Law & Order: SVU* at worst.

To quote an eight-year-old kid who once kicked me in the nuts, "They're all butts . . . and farts."

Let's whittle down what is essential to having a relationship with another person of either sex. You see, I think we need a checklist for the first year of a relationship. This would be known as the "Deal Breaker contract." Pretty standard stuff: for the first twelve months of the relationship there will be a number of violations deemed acceptable for termination at any time, regardless of the other person's feelings. I think this will solve two issues humans suffer from: (1) fear of that exit conversation and the crushing guilt that comes with it, and (2) after enough time living with this contract, it will leave more people comfortable with the idea of talking when they know it's not working out and less people stuck in shitty relationships that go on for years with no way of making them any better, no matter how many pity kids you have or how many times you try to give each other what you think you want. Like I said before, if you don't learn to talk to each other, not only will you never find out what your partner likes, but you'll also never know when things aren't going well. That's the only limbo I believe in: no babies who were never baptized, no innocent souls waiting for the rapture—just millions of people who can't speak to one another, thereby living as strangers and dying miserable.

Anyway, my checklist would break down like this.

Month One would be called the "free one." This is usually the month spent getting to know each other anyway, so it makes the most sense to commit the most flagrant fouls in this time period because there's a good chance the other person might consider them quaint or precocious—they still don't really *know* you! These could just be nervous quirks that might be ironed out over time! Besides, what's a month hurt? Anyone can afford a month—a month is not a decade. Give yourself a little time together. However, you need to pay attention to the reactions concerning your weirdness. If there is genuine laughter there, you might be okay; that's some shit you can keep doing if you like. But if it's met with things like nervous laughter, stifling silence, eye rolling, or a stone cold frown, you might want to add this to the list of things that will come up next month.

Month Two is the first shakedown. Everything from shoes left under the coffee table to how you go down on each other would fall under the microscope for scrutiny. Mind you, the sex will probably still be great fun at this point, so you have to be careful you don't fall in that trap. You have to keep your eyes on the two main queries: Is he or she worth continuing on with, and am I still having a good time? It could be that one month's business isn't long enough to get a bead on that kind of answer, but it's a good habit to get into, especially with the things you'll need to do in the coming months. So Month Two is a bit like a "story so far" moment: "Well, they haven't asked me to help them hide a body yet, but they *do* dip candy bars in peanut butter jars. Maybe they just need their own jars for dipping?" So far so good: the dialogue continues, and you get someone who isn't a murderer but really likes his peanut butter and chocolate.

Month Three is all about paying attention a little more. This is the time when you notice the subtleties, the nuances, and the little shit. Things like chewing fingernails instead of cutting them and panties in the sink—these are all fodder for discussion. Honestly, I don't know anyone who still puts their panties in the sink. But I've seen a pair of socks or two soaking in there, and it makes my teeth click. Discussions won't resume until Month Four, so this is more about taking notes and getting involved. It might just be that the sex is tapering off a little bit, so you'll have a little free time from the shackles and ball gags to put some pen to paper. Good thing too, because after a while those restraints chafe like a motherfucker. But don't worry: after enough time you start to develop calluses in the right places; then it's a matter of having your partner chew them . . . I'm sorry, I've said too much.

When Month Five commences, it's going to be quiet for a while. This is because this month is all about looking at your partner in the right light—that is, do they look okay naked, and are they pigging out on brutal calories? Are they keeping their figure? Does it matter if they have a tattoo on each thigh of a snail racing a turtle toward their cooter? Do they dimple up in spots, thereby freaking you out? This shit is important because it's all about paying attention to fluctuation. It's also the month you book that first dinner with each other's parents. It's good to have the face time, but there's a covert point as well: you know the old adage that women grow up to look like their mothers? This applies to dads as well. So get a look at the older versions and give a thought to the manifest destiny of your sex life.

Month Six: the two of you will have a State of the Union Address. This is when you air out any and all grievances: flirting with each other's friends, too much garlic in the food you cook, leaving the seat down in the bathroom, leaving the seat *up* in the bathroom, and so forth. It's also a good time to look at things that have been ignored from prior talks. Is he still clipping his toenails at the dinner table? Is she still bitching about her friends while you're watching your favorite show? Is he still smacking your ass too hard in bed? Is she still bitching about her friends while you're smacking her ass in bed? This is when you put it all on the line, because the next month is all about commonality, so get the state of affairs together quickly and try to stay on target.

Month Seven: What the fuck do you have in common? Have you started fighting more? Are you still talking? Do you still do stuff together? Time to look at the stuff you guys share, besides splitting headaches and those pints of Ben and Jerry's after a good movie. It doesn't have to be everything: everyone is and should rightly be different in a lot of ways. But look at certain things: Do you like the same movies or TV shows? Do you watch them together? Do you still go out together, or have you both gone back to hanging with friends? Do you talk about stuff other than what's right or wrong about your relationship, like whether or not the new *Star Wars* movies are going to be cool or if any of the Kardashians shoot ass fat into their faces in a desperate attempt to appear human? This is about relevance and relativity. No one wants to have the same conversations over and over.

Month Eight: time to talk about what's off limits and what might be on the table in the bedroom. Some people are up for anything, including the Twisting Pinky and the Dog in a Bathtub. Other folks aren't quite so open-minded or open-ended. You have to make sure the boundaries are in place. Anal? No? Fine and dandy. Oral? On both sides? Good call. Reverse Cowgirl? Thank God. Toe sucking? Too ticklish, huh? That's too bad but understood. It's only a pain in the ass—no pun intended—if you're too stifled by embarrassment. If you get past that and you *trust the person*, you can have it all. But that's one of the things about talking as much as you should—it can help develop that trust, in bed and out. Thusly, the more you get to know each other in life, the more you'll see the reflection of what they're like in the bedroom.

Months Nine and Ten are very simple: Have you tried living with each other? *Do* it, then see Month Eleven.

Month Eleven is the last ditch effort to find out what the fuck is going on. Is he a maniac about Trash Night and does he lose his cool if it's not on the curb before you both go to bed? Is she a nut if you're not romantic enough, like rose petals on the pillow every once in a while or a quiet lunch that ends in a make-out session by a lake? Is he faithful? Is she fucking around? Have you both started sizing up other people? This is the point of the system that maybe I didn't quite convey: at *any* point during this first year you can burn rubber for the horizon. Every month is a free one. If you haven't taken the opportunities afforded by these skull sessions to get out with dignity, it's your own fault. That's because after Month Twelve, you deserve the horseshit that comes your way if you're not happy anymore. Any schmuck, male or female, should fucking know within a *whole year* whether that other person is not The One, especially consider-ing you had *monthly chances* to bail with honor and intelligence. If you fuck it up in the next year, you deserve the punishment and hassles from everyone, because you're a nimrod who doesn't know what they want, and you shouldn't be allowed to date or romance anyone else for a year. Shit happens, douche pickle. Next time know yourself a little better instead of wasting every-one's time.

Let's get away from romance and all that frilly crap for a sec-ond and examine the relationships we all have with the nonhu-man. People fight weird issues with food. Some got hard-ons and rocky nipples for cars or money or expensive homes and what-not. Like my friend Leon used to say, "Ain't nothin' but nothin', motherfucker, now gimme a smoke." Well, he wasn't so much a friend as he was a dude who bought drugs from my friend's parents. But that's a great quote. It applies to so many different situations that I use it a lot when you need just the right amount of wit balanced with a decent dose of the word "motherfucker."

Food: some can handle it and others can't get their cravings under control. It's like being with addicts but the availability is everywhere, staring you in the face when you really need the respite. Some people binge eat and throw up, afflicted as they are with either bulimia or anorexia or body dysmorphia or any number of things that have become diseases over the last few decades. I try not to get too cynical about these problems because I know people who suffer at their hands. But I also know that there's more to the issue there, and just getting someone to stop that cycle is not enough. Some don't give a shit about getting help and would rather die than "look fat" in their mirrors. Others truly cannot get a grip on these gripping dilemmas. All these negative aspects over a substance we all need to stay alive. It hurts my head to think about it.

Is it a product of wanting for nothing? Is it that side effect of never needing a thing? Is it a hell that stems from the subtle opulence that comes from being free in a country that offers opportunities of every and any kind? Could be. Think about hoarders, those people who turn houses that were once homes into tombs sealed with belongings, important or pathetic alike. I understand there is a psychological angle there that, like bulimics and anorexics, takes time and therapy to work through, but growing up in houses that all had hints of hoarding going on, I can tell you right now it's no picnic being a nonhoarder in a hoarded household. There's a sadistic selfishness that goes along with it that no one wants to talk about—it's all about the people who can't stop filling their fucking houses with garbage and sales items. Nobody talks about the ones who never had a choice in the matter, who suffered because they couldn't bring friends home and, if they did, were made fun of constantly. Yes, life isn't fair. But work out how fair it is to people who have to deal with these sicknesses even though they're not the ones afflicted.

The gross underbelly are the people who just want more—not because they're hoarders but because they're greedy cunt lips who take advantage of people, glom onto their bank accounts, suck them dry, and move on to the next derelict with a bank roll. Yes, I understand that some of the people who get taken to town should've been a little more savvy and privy to the vixens and vacillators, the people running the grifts in the first place. But then again, can't people just not fucking *suck* as human beings once in a while? Is that too much to fucking ask? Is it too much to ask that people like each other for who they are and not what they have? Am I naïve about the nature of motherfuckers under Mother Nature's broken wings? Nah, fuck that. People have just as much capacity to be good as they do to be shit. It's a choice. People make choices. So they need to make better fucking choices.

Then there's that strange borderland of religions and our "relationships" with the unknown. Oh Boy Howdy, everybody's got a god these days. Everybody's got the inside track on the better end and the bitter truth. Everybody has a different book full of fun facts on how to have a better understanding or relationship with their gods, every one of them. The crazy bit of business here is that you'd *think* this would bring people into a better relationship with each other. But nope. Because everyone's so fucking smart these days, they think they know better than everyone else what these books are really saying about those gods, and their interpretations are different because they *know* they're right. Too many prophets, not enough flocks—this is what happens when dumb creatures get it in their heads that there's divinity out there somewhere. No one's on the same pages of the same books about the same gods. Guess what? That's how wars start, children.

Isn't it scary to anyone else that as much as we ridicule or feel pity for the ancients, after thousands of years we're still having the same arguments about gods that don't exist? Think about that before you pat yourselves on the back too hard for being able to program a VCR or change your fucking ringtones.

In the end relationships of all kinds define who we are inside, the one nobody sees or talks to. They are reflections of the unspoken soul because, as hard as it is for some of you to open up, who you inevitably spend time with is a good indication of who you are or want to be. They say you can judge a person by the company they keep, but what they don't say is that you should dig a little deeper to understand how you and the company you keep get along in life. There are infinite lines of dialogue and energy that can go back and forth between the masses, and just because one person is a douche doesn't mean his friend is too. However, maybe that friend has moments of douche baggery when he or she is *with* that friend, doing things or acting in ways they would never think of with their other acquaintances.

The way we approach relationships with *anything* these days is to overdo it. No one knows how to find the right balance and go with the flow. Everyone has to get *exactly* what they want *exactly* when they need it from *exactly* the right person or food or thing or fucking whatever. People are obsessed with fulfilling their needs before anything else in life. The selfishness makes for a million "butts and farts" running around, convinced they'll never be happy unless they get *precisely what they want*. I don't know whether it's what personal freedom persuades us to think we need or it's just because, with so many things around us so readily available, like information and technology, we have developed an addiction to instant gratification. Either way, we're all a bunch of spoiled brats wandering this galactic pebble, yelling and arguing when we don't get what we want.

Life's not the Internet, fuckholes.

Life doesn't sway or give when you try to force it to give you what you crave, whether it's a lover or a liver transplant. Because of life, you learn to roll with the punches, even if you have to take a few head shots before you find out the hard way. Satisfaction only breeds selfishness: it's not a bad thing per se, but depending on what you're pursuing, it can be anything from the death of desire to the destroyer of the ability to dream, if I can paraphrase slightly. When you always get what you want, you build up a tolerance—in the sense of an illness—against appreciation. More importantly, you become intolerant to anything, perceived or real, that feels like a setback or a loss. This is how we are meant to develop as people and expand on our inner compassion and empathy. When we lose that, forget about relationships; we are *fucked* as a species. We will be headed for the day when we're just finely dressed monkeys assaulting each other with shit (*literal* shit) filled with gravel and cherry pits.

Don't get mad at me: *you're* the ones who look like brown stains in the world's underwear. I'm just pointing it out. You know why people don't get married and stay together anymore? It's because they think their momentary lust is love, and when that lust burns itself dry, they want out to find someone else. You know why so many people are fucking obese these days— and I don't mean by those bullshit universal standards you get when you go to the doctor; I mean based on the eye test. It's because no one can stand the thought of not being able to eat anything and everything as much as possible all the fucking time. Humanity has run out of willpower. Humanity has run out of patience. It has turned into Gollum, stroking his Precious in the caverns and eating what he kills. Our backs have arched and our hearts have gone black. We want everything and we want it *now*. Never mind that we don't know what real love is: we want love *now*. Never mind that we can't handle food or drugs or booze or sex or anything in moderation. We want it all *now*. Never mind that we don't know how to make ourselves truly happy because the only way we know how to be happy is to get what we want *now*.

Give it to us *now*.

We fucking want it *now*.

You want the truth?

"Yes, we want the truth *now*."

You all fucking suck at life.

NOW . . .

Deal with it or change.

CHAPTER 8

CHILDREN OF CLODS

Twas standing in line at the airport in Columbus, Ohio, wondering what in bloody fucking hell was taking so goddamn long, when the thought occurred to me that *someone's going to run that kid over and I'm going to laugh.*

Let me explain.

The Boss (aka the wife) and I had flown into Ohio so I could get my ass handed to me: it was, of course, the occasion of the Third Annual Rock 'n' Roll Roast, being held on Rock on the Range weekend, and the honoree—I say that with only a hint of sarcasm—was yours truly: me. Ostensibly it would be painless in a very painful way, and that was indeed the case. However, the event was sold out, we were able to raise some great money for a foundation called MusiCares (which helps addicts in the music industry get treatment and so much more), and everyone had a really good time. Well, when I say "everyone," I actually mean anyone who didn't get their feelings hurt. Sebastian Bach did throw a full Starbucks coffee at Don Jamieson while the comic was *still* at the podium, but other than that very isolated incident, it was a great success. My friend Clown drank his own pee and threatened everyone with a giant butcher knife—all in all, it was an atypical Thursday.

After the aforementioned festivities, The Boss and I woke up ready to head back home the following day. We packed up, grabbed lunch, and headed to the Port Columbus International Airport with time to spare. This is where we pick up the action because even though she and I are quite efficient when it comes to travel of any kind, sometimes the cards are just stacked against us. We'd checked in quite quickly, but then we found ourselves languishing in a line so unnecessarily slow it was like trying to drink tree sap with a hundred-foot paper straw. This is how slow it was: we were second in line and stood there for forty minutes. There was a man traveling alone in front of us and a family of three at the counter. Forty minutes. That's no exaggeration. It was the "bag drop" line—we didn't even need to get our tickets. There was no one behind us for twenty-five of those minutes. Even by a turtle's standards, that is extraordinarily slow.

One of the reasons this line was abysmally slothful was because of the family who was "being helped" at the counter. The family consisted of a man, a woman, and their son, whom I assume was two years old. Between them they had eight fucking pieces of luggage. The lady behind the counter was doing her best to help them with a smile, but I watched them *twice* have to repack their stupid suitcases to save money on weight distribution. Everyone involved seemed clueless, including the man who was in front of us in line; he missed two separate opportunities to get helped by someone at a different position because he wasn't paying attention. It was a torturous blend of waiting, frowning, and gritting my teeth. Most days I have the patience of a man waiting for sainthood. That particular Friday was not going to help my clean-play record.

While I waited, I began to pay complete attention to the two-year-old boy screaming "DA!" every two seconds. He was latched into a stroller from the 1980s, the kind that looks like an elderly aunt uses it to bring home groceries on Sunday afternoon. This kid was not exactly stoked about being strapped to this contraption, so he was flailing about and playing that "fun" game in which he drops whatever it is he's holding, waits for mom or dad to pick it up and give it back to him, and then immediately drops it again, a little farther away. The best part of that game is when mom or dad doesn't want to play anymore, so they hold onto the item. This produces a shriek from the little tyrant that is held for an inordinate amount of time until one of the parents breaks down and gives the item back in a fit of exasperation . . . and the cycle begins all over again. This went on for a while before the father, a man in his pajamas trying to appear authoritative, made a split-second decision.

He let the kid out of his stroller.

This was when that thought at the top of the chapter popped into my head like a rabid bastard cruising accident sites. For ten minutes I watched this kid wander off on his own—A TWO-YEAR-OLD BOY WHO COULD BARELY WALK—screaming "DA!" for everyone and their mom to hear. He would wander off into "traffic"—the constant stream of weary travelers running at light speed. Every time he got farther and farther away, and the father would have to stop what he was doing at the counter and go get him, bring him back, and set him down . . . only to have him wander off again. There were hundreds of people walking by, all at a healthy clip because—shock and horror!—they were in an airport in a hurry! After the fortieth time I saw this kid nearly get run down by air travelers, I said out loud, "Someone's going to run that kid over and I'm going to laugh." My wife gave me a look of surprise for a second, then thought about the situation, and reluctantly agreed. I turned around at one point and the kid was just *gone*. Dad ran away from the counter in the direction of his last known whereabouts, and while his back was turned, the kid came stumbling out of the women's restroom, loudly calling that same battle cry.

At some point you kind of have to ask yourself: How the hell do I get outsmarted and outmaneuvered by a kid who's only been alive for two years? Then again, this is the modern malady—a horrid example of how we, the adults, are letting down them, the young, in a feeble attempt to avoid hurting children's feelings. If the parents aren't doing that, they're trying to fit in with their kids and their friends. If they're not doing *that*, they reside in the area of ignoring everything about the children unless they can benefit the parents' meaningless existence in some way, usually when other dickheads like themselves are paying attention. All of these reasons and more are why, after careful examination and due process, I have crunched some numbers and arrived at the following conclusion:

The modern parent is a fucking asshole.

I mean that sincerely. I mean that as surely as when I say "There is no god" or "I hope I never hear Avril Lavigne's voice ever again." The modern parent is a dick bag who has been shell-shocked by the media and other fuck-face caregivers. On the one hand, some have been pushed into thinking that if they don't do *everything* with their kids, they're neglectful bastards. So these people do everything with them. It's one thing to do some stuff with your kids, like run errands or fit in some quality hang time.

However, some of the shit they get up to is out and out obsessive, compulsive, and borderline mother-fucking abusive.

On the other hand, if they're not smothering, they're *not* smothering—by which I mean they're not doing anything at all. They treat their children like window dressing, something to fluff up when company comes over or when friends ask after them. They pay just enough attention to answer a barrage of questions if the authorities get involved. Other than that, they can't be bothered. They barely know the kid's middle name, and *they* are the ones who came up with it. I can't tell you how many times I've watched a lonely kid just walk around a park while their mom—and it's usually the mom, blowing up *that* particular image—sits on her ass and texts or tweets or fucking cruises Facebook for someone to cheat with. It's pathetic. So I can't tell the lesser of the two evils: the ones who do fuck all or the ones who fucking do it all. Either way your kids get the shit end of the dipstick, and that might just come back on you a thousandfold.

If I had a nickel for every time I've seen a parent do something fucking stupid that involves their kid or multiple kids, I wouldn't need to write these books. Hell, I could even retire from my other job as a singer for those bands I'm in and live comfortably for the rest of my life. I mean, holy cheddar tits . . . leashes? You're walking your kids on leashes? Do you keep their fucking water bowls clean too? Did you buy them a bed, or do they sleep on a shitty blanket? Why not go all the way—when they're old enough, have them spayed! I'm sure they won't mind, and at least you'll know definitively that teenage pregnancy won't be an issue. If you're going to treat your kid like a fucking pet, then we're all going to judge you. You knew it when you bought that sorry excuse for a parenting tool in the collars section at Babies 'R' Us; now sit in it and shut up.

I don't know what's worse, honestly—the leash or the ways that parents try to integrate their children into their "exercise program" without looking like a tool. I have never seen one kid who was stoked to be strapped into a "sport stroller" and shoved down the street because mommy's got a fat ass and needs to burn it off. Another example is when daddy puts all those protective pads on the four-year-old and drags him or her along for aggressive rollerblading—all while not wearing a shirt. Mind you, I don't have any problem with people getting in shape; I work out myself as much as possible. God forbid you just have someone watch your kid for a second. But you just got to make sure everyone knows you're a good parent: "She hasn't left my side! See? I'm paying attention! Are you kidding, she *loves* the jostling and the motion sickness!" Lady, you're a prick. Kids get sick enough as it is without giving them a new way to do so.

That brings me to my next scathing accusation—and none of you are going to like it. Being a father myself, you need to understand the earnestness with which I hurl at you the following utterance: your fucking kids *suck* . . . and it's all your fault, parents.

The time has come to bear down and chomp on the truth. Certain lines should never be crossed. It's like the bringer of the brood cannot stand that there's a younger, faster version ready for the big time. Either we're treating our fucking kids like accessories for recreation and exercise or we're trying to act like we're their age, putting up a front to compete for attention. Yay, Mom. I'm sure your daughter loves that you want people to think you're sisters, because nothing makes a teenager or a twenty-something feel better about herself than being compared to a woman in her fifties. It's like you're *trying* to raise a hooker with issues. Oh, and one more thing: stop trying to bang your daughter's boyfriends. That's just grossly inappropriate.

BOOM! Just like that, I made it awkward, so we'll get away from that . . . for now.

You know who I feel sorry for? Those kids in Baby Bjorns, swinging around with the worst look of baby bum-out known to mankind. I've seen fathers covered in those things: two rigs, two kids, and fistfuls of dry cereal, shoving them into empty mouths as they make their way down the streets of a city teeming with filth and fodder. He's feeding one like the clip of a machine gun and the other he's just reaching blindly over one shoulder, desperately trying to find the kid's mouth while not running into shit like telephone poles, mailboxes, and other human beings. The whole time he's jogging. Kids jutting from his back and gut, Cheerios falling through hapless fingers—and he's jogging. That's the reason he's out and about: he's not taking the kids for a stroll, and he's not bringing them with him while he runs to the store; he's exercising so the soccer moms of the world look at him and think, "Look at that healthy hunk of extramarital possibility." In reality people regard him as the idiot in the Under Armour who's on the verge of abusing his kids. Sorry, Jim Fix Jr.—nobody likes a moron who multitasks with his brood.

Having kids does some crazy shit to your psyche, your identity, and your sense of satisfaction. The thing I learned when I had my kids is that for the rest of my life it's not all about me anymore. You get moments, of course. Everybody needs to unplug from the parental mainframe and get a little sugar somewhere else occasionally. There's nothing wrong with that, and you shouldn't be ashamed. However, this is an age of extremes; the common human has no idea what balance is all about and therefore does nothing in moderation. So the usual shit becomes unusually ridiculous: you get the absolute absence or the complete control, meaning you're either all over your kids or you have no clue where they are and you don't care. No wonder this generation is fucking angry—I don't blame them. I would be too if their choices were "shit" and "shit with a hair in it." "Hey, kids! It's 10 p.m. . . . do you know where *your* parents are?"

Then there are the new-wave parents—the hep cats with their unfounded theories—who believe it's okay to let the kids raise themselves as a way to hasten their individuality. These hippies think that by allowing a toddler to basically fend for his or her self, the kid is going to get it together faster than the average Disney kid. On the one hand, it makes a little sense and I've seen evidence that it can make a difference with that approach—we have friends with a young boy who is further ahead of the curve than most teenagers I know. But you have to be specially equipped to do this; in other words, you yourselves have to know what the fuck you're doing. You can't be fuck-ups and use this "Sedona Method" as an excuse to just not put the work in. Trust me: there will be repercussions.

There is a couple I am very close to who have a wolverine for a child. We'll call him Seamus to protect him from future admonishment. I don't know whether it's because this couple is just not on the ball themselves or because putting in the work is too much of a hassle, but after four years as "parents," they have found themselves raising a tiny barracuda. When you go to their house, you immediately understand that a maniac runs the place. There is food on the floor and the furniture. Mad scrawlings appear on the walls like pictographs from a race that died out aeons ago. Broken shit is everywhere. Then you hear the roar in the distance and the sound of little malicious feet running in your direction. This is when, if you're in the know, you immediately protect your nuts. Seamus is coming, and whether he likes you, hates you, or has never met you before, he is going to run head first into your crotch or swing a baseball bat at your balls.

This kid makes a prison riot at Arkham look like a school field trip. He walks up and tries to take food off your plate. He gets his hands on your possessions like your phone, and if he can't play with it, he'll try to break it. He screams until you let him get his way. He will hit you until you let him get his way. This kid is either going to become the school bully or is going to get his ass handed to him on a regular basis, and I'm here to fucking tell you that after a point, it's not his fault—it's his parents' fault. They didn't teach him shit about boundaries, self-soothing, or honest patience. They did none of that shit, and now they are suffering for it. The child runs that house like Stalin in the fifties: long hours, short tempers, and devoid of pity. Then they try to bitch to me about what a hard job it is being a parent. As a friend, I tell them straight up, "It's your fault, you dumb ass! *You* did this! *You* are the parent. If you don't at least lay down the law, how is this child supposed to know any better? You don't teach him shit—how is he supposed to know shit?"

To be fair, they haven't asked me over in a long time.

But then again, why the hell would I go over there? Why, so I can walk in the door and constantly be on my guard against a kid who thinks he's a tiny ball-busting battering ram? Fuck *all* that shit, and I wouldn't even *think* about taking my kids over there because what if that shit's contagious? Maybe it's *28 Days Later* and it's a juvenile equivalent to the Rage Virus? I can hear your heads shaking in anger, and I will at least acknowledge the ridiculousness of that thought. But I'm a father, and I ain't taking any fucking chances. That shit could be like lice or cooties: once it's in your skin, no amount of washing will kill the talk at the jungle gyms. Horrid business, that: just imagine the conversations over milk at lunch. "I heard Judy got the ragers, poor girl. She was so young . . . " It could happen. Fuck YOU, IT COULD HAPPEN.

I have a terrible habit that I'll fill you in on about me: I get so frustrated with Griffin's friends that, whether their parents are around or not, I go out of my way to scare the fuck out of them so they never misbehave around me again, sometimes leading them to never want to come back to our house any time in the future. Thankfully they still like hanging out with Griff because he's such a rad kid, so they invite him over for sleepovers and birthday parties. But they all hesitate the second they step foot in Casa de Taylor. Rightfully so too—not that I can't be a fun dad, mind you. I always enjoy hanging out with the boys, and we'll do shit like play catch in the backyard or I'll take every-body to the movies. But they also know they don't get away with the same shit in my house. Plus, if I don't catch it, Stephanie does, and she makes me look like a Salvation Army Santa Claus. Her other nickname is The Hulk: I don't really think I need to say any more. You get the picture.

Griffin has two specific friends whom, when I see them or they come to our house, I immediately have to remind myself not to go off on them because they're kids and they don't know any better. One is the boy called "Milt," whom I mentioned in the first chapter. Milt is a lot like Griff—small for his age but with a ton of energy and imagination. Those boys are thick as thieves. But I don't think Griff picks up on some of the stuff this kid Milt does. If he did, I don't think they'd be friends. Let me tell you about the first time Milt stayed overnight at our house. Steph was out of town, and I had some friends staying with us, so the house was full. I went to pick Griff up from school, and he came bounding out with Milt. They charged up to me and said, "Milt's spending the night because his parents said it was okay."

Now, the first thing wrong with this is that neither of the two asked *me* whether it was okay, and it became clear that Milt had told his family he was going to Griff's for the night. I scolded the two of them, saying it's not a plan until you talk to me about it. I let it slide; Griff doesn't get to have a lot of friends over—most of his friends' parents are scared of me. We all jumped into the Range Rover and headed home.

Then Milt's phone rang.

First of all, let's talk about that. Why would a preteen need a smartphone? Why would you let that kid take it to school? If you're the one who picks him up, there's no need for that, and any calls they need to make at school should come from the school's phone. I see more and more kids with these damn things. I'm sure some of them are warranted but not *all* of them. That shit just drives me fucking banana shits. Anyway, Milt's phone rang. This is where the fun begins.

Apparently he had *not* discussed this with the people picking him up from school, and I'd basically driven off with a child who was not my own. Thoughts of kidnapping charges flew through my head as I asked Milt, "Dude, did you even *ask*? Or did you just think you could call and everything would be all right?" It turned out he'd spoken to one parent, who then went to work without telling anyone else in the extended family, people who were, at that moment, combing the school grounds for this kid. I got on the phone and apologized to his aunt and asked whether she'd like me to bring him back. After she replied that as long as he had permission from his parents, it was okay, I gave Milt's phone back to him and we went home.

Once we arrived back at the house I announced we'd be having tacos that night, much to the delight of Griff—not only would we be having tacos, we'd be having Taco Bell, and Griff's favorites: those Doritos taco things. I don't get it, but okay—he likes them, so to each his own. Griff let out a shout of "Yes!" Milt paused, wrinkled his nose, and, like an old man at a restaurant, sighed and said, "Yeah . . . tacos aren't really my *thing*." I looked at this kid like he was a sasquatch—what kid doesn't like fucking tacos? But I swallowed whatever angry retort I had on deck and replied with, "Well, Milt, tacos are what we're having, and tacos are what you're going to get." He smirked at me and walked away.

Do you know what that little motherfucker did next?

Milt went outside, called his grandmother, and made her bring him Long John Silver's. Read that sentence again because we're going to talk about all the things that are wrong about it. This kid went away from earshot, phoned his grandmother *who was at work*, and made her go to Long John Silver's so he could eat what *he* wanted. Milt lives on the other side of town, and his grandmother, I later learned, works even farther away than that. So Milt, like it was the most natural thing in the world, called his grandmother to complain that he didn't *want* tacos; he wanted popcorn shrimp. He wanted what he wanted. Now, mind you, I understand there is very little nutritional difference between Long John Silver's and Taco Bell. I was fully prepared to buy fast food for my son; I'm not judging on the fast food front. I am, however, judging all over the fucking place on the fact that this kid made one phone call to a woman who was busy at work to complain that he wasn't going to get his way, and instead of that woman telling her grandson to shut up and buck up, she left work, went to a drive-thru, picked it up, and brought it to him. Now look at the situation: Whose fault is it? Is it Milt's? That little shit pissed me off so bad with that move that I haven't let Griff invite him back over. I know: I'm older and I know better, but I'm also just a big enough asshole to hold a grudge against a little dick nose who hasn't even hit puberty yet.

Or is it his grandmother's fault? I've been to their house—not inside but to drop him off—and I know he's not an only child. I know he's probably getting just enough attention. So why in this entire sweet world would you immediately give in to a summons like that? What part of you thinks that's an okay thing to do? Why in the fuck would that kid think it's okay to do something like that unless . . . he's done it before? If he thinks that's acceptable and not a complete fucking waste of everybody's time, how do you think he got there? I'll tell you exactly how he got there: because he's a fucking *brat*, spelled "B-R-A-Tea Bags." That little shit is going to grow up with such a sense of entitlement that it's going to collapse back on his parents, who I am sure are just working hard to take care of a fairly decent-sized family. But someday Milt's going to go rogue on them—I've seen it before. Because of the way they've raised him, he's not going to be ready for the punch in the nuts that life in general has to offer him. He's going to get broken down: on the playground, between classes in high school, at job interviews, and so forth. Milt might not make it . . . all because his parents were too scared of disappointing him to tell him *NO*.

"No" is a good fucking thing to have in your parental golf bag. I tell Griff *No* all the time. Sometimes I'm a pushover and I let him do his thing, but I also know when is the right time and when it's time to shut it down for the night. You *have* to have that valve in the machine because if you don't, you end up looking like a complete fuckface—making up an excuse at work so you can take your shitty grandkid some popcorn shrimp, all because he's too fucking cool for tacos. Sorry—I'm still raw about that. I wished to God I could say I've learned to like Milt a little more, but I really don't. In fact, I've said some shit to him that my friends, all of which were standing right there, had to leave the room because they couldn't believe I just said that shit to a child. Nothing bad—get that out of your heads. Just some subtle shit that he might think about later and go, "Wow, Mr. Taylor was a *dick* . . . " Then again, maybe he'll be smart enough to go, "Wow, Mr. Taylor was right—I *was* a dick . . . "

Only time will tell, as the Nelson brothers sang long ago . . .

The second of Griff's friends is a little more complex to talk about. Instead of too much attention from his parents, he doesn't really get any, mainly because his parents are so wrapped up in their own lives and mutual drama that they don't really do a lot with him or the rest of the family. It's painful to watch, and we all do our best to fill in some of these blanks, but at the end of it all, there's only so much we can do. When he's over, we treat him like family, which means I get on him just as bad as I get on Griffin. I like to think it does a little good—having grown up that way myself, it's a wonderful thing to feel like there's some stability out there somewhere. I spent a *lot* of time when I was younger with my best friend Darold's family before I moved to Des Moines to live with my grandmother. They were much like my wife's family now, and they all provide me with the same thing: comfort in chaos and love.

Look, I'm not a monster and I'm not judging everybody. I've certainly done my share of spoiling over the years. There was a period when Griff was quite young that, because I felt so much guilt from being on the road all the time, I'd take him toy shopping constantly. Maybe because of that, every once in a while he expects things he hasn't earned or just wants something, whether it's his birthday, Christmas, or not. That's my fault, and I'm doing what I can to change that. But I also know my son—he has the biggest heart of anyone I know sometimes. This is a kid who likes to buy toys for other kids on his own birthday. This is a kid so sensitive sometimes that if he sees another kid crying when we're out somewhere, he worries about that kid long after we've gone away from them. I'm not worried about him on that level because I know his empathy for others will always keep him out of the spoiled rotten category. All kids have their moments in that area, no matter how you raise them. They'll eventually grow out of it. You've got to look past that to how they are as the people they are going to become. There's your future adult you need to keep an eye on.

Parents, I care. I really do. But growing up the way I did, I will tell you one thing: I'm fucking watching and taking notes too. I grew up an amateur criminal, so I know the signs. I grew up an addict, so I know where to look for that shit too. You all need to do better jobs or at least get another job to help with bail money. If you look at the way the world has gone these days, you know it's a matter of time before something breaks, and I can lay a lot of that at your feet. But this is the age of excuses. Today it's not the parents' fault for some of this aberrant behavior—it's somebody else's entirely. If Junior gets shit grades, it's not the kid or the parents—it's the teachers. If Junior gets picked up for shoplifting or drugs, it's not his or her fault nor is it the parents—it's their friends or society. All of these excuses are horse apples, and I've been hearing them since before I could fire up a fart with a yellow Bic lighter. So guess what: you know why your kids take no responsibility? Because you don't take any responsibility yourselves. You're never at fault, so why should they be?

It all starts at home. The moment your child leaves your house they are a walking representative of how your household rolls. If your kid is even-keeled and ready to help, usually that's a sign of a decent upbringing. But if your kid can't be bothered to do any-thing anywhere other than complain and mope and bitch or call you to bring them some fucking McNuggets (I am so sorry, but, motherfucker, that *still* fucking bothers me . . . Milt . . .), that shit is *your fault*. Sit in it. Own it. Do something about it. I don't care. But don't pass the buck, you prick. It's your fucking fault.

Let's talk about something horribly inappropriate now.

Most babies are really ugly, man.

Sorry, that shit is true. I've seen infants who look so bad, you know for certain they are *never* going to grow into their faces. So it's everything I can do to keep from losing my shit when I hear parents speak glowingly about how beautiful this ugly-ass cherub is. Oh brother—seriously? You don't see what's wrong there? His nose is backward! Her eye looks like it drifted down the side of her face, and that's her *best* feature! Your kid looks so fugly I want to call Ghostbusters. They say beauty is in the eye of the beholder. I'm here to tell you plainly: the beholder can also be fucking blind. I've seen cuter kittens thrown into sacks and tossed into rivers. Y'all need to get your damn prescriptions checked, and I'm talking eyeglasses and medicines, whatever they may be. Jesus on a skiff . . .

I've had to walk away from my friends when they ask ques-tions they know damn well I'm going to answer honestly. There's *too* much truth, you hear me? I have a friend with a daughter who looks very severe in the face. If I were forced to testify in court, I would swear the kid looks like a popular *Harry Potter* character. She asked me point-blank one day whether I thought she was pretty. I didn't know what to do, so I turned to a simple series of movements I have dubbed the "nonoffensive commit-tal." Next time you find yourself in a *sticky* situation (snicker), try this shit on for size.

It starts with a narrowing of the eyes, like you're trying to see something that's too far away. For those of you with perfect eyesight, pretend you've sniffed out a cat box and you're trying not to smell while you breathe. Then slowly but surely—and this is key—SWIVEL YOUR HEAD in a languid manner, fast enough that it looks like you're nodding yes but slow enough that deep down you *know* you're shaking your head no. As you're doing this, you have to give a sort of "Mmmmm . . . " sound, which *could* mean yes or could mean no. All of these things really rely on whatever the other person is looking for in an answer. If they want positive reinforcement, they will see a person emphatically agreeing with them. If they feel like the kid could use a "facelift," they'll see someone else who sees the problem. All kids are beautiful . . . on the inside. Some of them look like they've been initiated into a gang recently. I know, right!? That shit *is* fucked up! But you don't know whether I'm talking about your kid or not . . .

And you might never know.

The fucked up thing is that's not even the worst thing that me and mine say about your kids. Should I tell you how bad it gets? Shit, might as well—no one in the fucking world would believe it. How many of you are familiar with football pools? You know what I mean: you chuck your money in the kitty, pick a winner, and pray that something goes well for your team. This can be applied to any sport and has been for many years now. People make out like bandits. You get enough people chucking money in the pot, that shit can look quite tempting. It makes you do some crazy shit. It makes you consider applying the same stakes . . . to whether certain kids are going to grow up a certain way.

I know, but I've routinely warned you all that I am *not* a good person. I don't know why you keep coming back here . . .

Yes, my friends and family and I bet on whether specific kids are going to grow up to do things like, oh I don't know . . . rob a bank, fail in school, wear another person's skin as pajamas—you know, normal shit that kids grow up to accomplish. I've got $20 bucks on a kid right now who I am convinced is going to stir someone's guts up with a paint scraper. Trust me: if you saw this kid and talked to him—*or her*—you'd never fall asleep unless you had a few locked doors between you and he—*or she*. Yeah, it's a fucked-up thing to bet on, the absolute collapse of a child's potential and sanity. But hey . . . football season only lasts so long. And if most of you didn't suck at raising your kids, I wouldn't have a reason to bet on their almost inevitable social destruction.

This chapter has of course gone off the rails (that seems to be the way I write books), right on schedule . . . get it? Rails? Schedule? IT'S A TRAIN JOKE! And this is a chapter about sucky kids! Right? I know, it's *flawless*! Well, I had to say something to make this seem more like humor and less like my manifesto against the younger folks of the human genome. Seriously, I don't hate all children—just yours, really. They're all little boogers dedicated to ripping up your shit, hitting you in the face, and leaving enough food in their wake that cockroaches around the world consider your home the Tahiti of the insect world, with manna from heaven and streets made of candy, or in this case, old Cap'n Crunch and slivers of turkey sandwiches. I'm no mind reader, but I'm going to guess that you didn't buy that house to attract vermin from any and all continents and feed their millions of babies. So why do you let your fucking kid get away with that shit?

I've been watching this all, and it's getting worse with each round of generations and kin: people too busy fucking and procreating to think beforehand about whether that's a good idea. Then when they have those kids, they don't know what the fuck they're doing and get super-butt-hurt when you deign to offer some advice, something like, "You might want to keep your kid from putting his mouth on that dumpster, Marge . . . " You'd think the smell would've warned the kid away from trying to taste the trash, but I think some kids are just dicks so they can prove they exist, even if that means risking their tongues to the gods of garbage. Now don't get me wrong: I'm *going* to laugh. But I won't like it.

Part of being a parent is of course keeping the kid alive until he or she can do it themselves, but the other part is teaching them *not* to be a fucking asshole, and I'm sorry, but you're all becoming very fucking derelict in those goddamn duties. I am not condoning physical punishment—God knows, I took enough of that shit to last my kids and *their* kids several lifetimes—but there is nothing wrong with an occasional swat on the behind to remind them that there are consequences for bad behavior. I don't give a shit what the fucking hippies say; it's not abuse to give your kids a spanking. I think it's worse to raise a spoiled little shit. Then again, if you raise your kid right, you won't have the need to give them a swat. These are all parts of being a parent—not parking your kid like a bike at the park so you can go shopping.

Every time—and I mean *every time*—I am away from my kids my guts are torn up, I have a hard time sleeping, and I never feel totally happy. Seeing as I'm away from them a lot, you get the picture on what it's like to be C motherfucking T. But that little time I get with them I try to be the best dad I can, whether that means playing with them, teaching them, or keeping them in check. This shit is hard, man. It's not easy being a *good* parent;

it's a lot of work. That's why not everybody takes the time to do it. Sure, they'll fuck like bunnies and have the kid so they can post shitty selfies with their baby in the background, but they won't raise it right, feed it right, treat it right, and they won't give a fucking shit because it has nothing to do with *them*. Selfishness is breeding our children into ungrateful monsters, and there's only so much I can do about it.

But you just wait. Someday you're going to turn around because you need something from your kids or someone else's kids. You'll show up at a store or the DMV or the airport (fuck that place) or Long John Silver's (FuckING MILT!), and you know what you're going to get? You're going to get a fucking adult who acts like a teenager because they weren't taught early on to respect and be responsible. You're going to need them to help you, like really help you. You're going to need someone to take care of you. You're going to need someone smart and savvy and supportive because you can't do a lot for yourself anymore. You're going to look to this generation, a generation raised through glass and watered on pitiful liquids, and ask for help. You're going to ask them to be people and act like people who care. You're going to need empathy. You're going to need intelligence. You're going to need some fight other than fists and madness. You're going to think about how you raised your kids and how your friends raised theirs, and you're going to get worried. You'll hope and pray that things will be okay.

You're going to need help. You're going to need your kids to be someone that, unfortunately, you didn't raise them to be. You're going to need them to be stronger and better than you raised them to be. You're going to close your eyes, whisper "please," and turn around, reaching out with a hand that needs desperately to feel warmth, safety, and strength. You're going to need that help from your son or daughter or son and daughter. You're going to turn around.

No one's going to be there.

And it will be your fault.

Chapter 9

What the Fuck
Is That Noise?

I may blow a million minds right now, but I have a confession to make. We're talking worldwide exclusive here. So here goes . . .

I fucking *despise* the show *Glee*.

Seriously, I fucking hate it. Now before you go off on some crazy tangent about how they depict diversity, acceptance, and a positive view on how young people can get along together in a perfect world, it has nothing to do with that, although the acting is mediocre and some of the ways they've deified the Monteith kid are gross and inappropriate. No, my level of maximum vitriol has nothing to do with any of that; it's what they do to the music. Never mind the originals—that music is pure trash and the fact that some of those songs are hits is a travesty to the term "hits"; it's the way they treat other people's material. The way they auto-tune, "modernize," and flagrantly neuter some of these songs is a fucking joke. The only good by-product of the "*Glee* bump," as it's known in certain circles, is that the artists who *wrote* those songs get a surge on iTunes and record sales. The irony is that many of the children who watch that show don't have a fucking clue that the cast is ruining songs that were written maybe ten to twenty years before they were born. But listening to the "teenage" performers destroy these classics is like watching Wolverine trying to detail an Aston Martin DB7 with his claws out. I can only thank Satan that by the time this is published, *Glee* will be no more. As I've always said, good riddance to bad rubbish.

Many of you are very familiar with my opinions about music. Well, if I never write another book again, I am going to take this opportunity to really present how I feel about the notion of "popular music" today. Hopefully this will put an end to the constant questions I am bombarded with in every interview I have ever done.

Every day I am assaulted by garbage. I wake up in the morning, turn on the TV, and instantly get stung by a million mediocre bees in the form of crappy writing, weak synth pop, gargling vocals, and nasal so-called rock 'n' roll. It all sounds the same: every song has the familiar quirky keyboard/acoustic "riff," a moaning attempt at a verse by college dropouts, and a falsetto melody disguised as a hook that serves as the big "chorus." They may be in different keys and performed by different bands, but EVERY SONG IS THE SAME. And it gets worse: every fucking song is designed to get you to buy something. That's because every "popular" song you hear is attached to car insurance, real estate websites, Apple products, expensive headphones, tablets, auto dealers, and anything else that's trying to take more of your money. Commercials are the new music videos now, and every channel on television is MTV. It's genius and it's crass and it's slowly but surely killing my soul.

If you watch closely, most commercials that feature these songs have the band name and song title embedded at the end like the list of stipulations assigned to a Labor Day weekend car sale. That's how they get away with it: the bands convince themselves that it's the best way to get their "art" to the people. They sell out their integrity, if they ever fucking had any, to get a quick little taste of what might have been before the age of the Internet, the truest killer of giants. Because of the Internet, every way that bands could make a living righteously was destroyed or dismantled. Record sales, videos . . . hell, even live shows in a way—these were all supplanted with the push of a button and the click of a mouse. Suddenly everything you worked for could be downloaded illegally. Instantly music videos had no safe haven on TV anymore, and even though YouTube has given them a new life, it wasn't the same. The structure had been scheduled for demolition, and no one cared.

Then those clever little Indie hipster bands figured out they could help shill for The Man and get their crappy half-assed single on the telly by licensing it to the corporations, thereby making them all neither independent nor hip. Their ideals became transparent, their style became a crock, and it opened the floodgates for hundreds of copycats willing to fake a genre to get ahead. The band Fun won a Grammy award for an album that had two singles featured in at least eight commercials, and that's just off the top of my head. Never mind the fact that band won Best Rock Album (they're about as rock 'n' roll as Pat Boone). Pop songs are nothing more than hamburgers and high-end shoes now, commodities used to scrape for the last thing we hold precious in the world—money. Everything's about money.

Everything's about capital. Everything is afforded a price tag that we can't possibly afford in the end. It's fucking disgusting, and the fact that it's my industry, my way of life, the only thing I've ever been good at or cared about in the world makes me want to pull open the planet's mouth and throw up into it uncontrollably. I am ashamed to be a singer. I am embarrassed to be a songwriter. What's worse is that I don't really know what to do about it.

No one's listening. No one cares. People just accept it as is. The art was discarded a long time ago. I sit, drinking my coffee and scratching my ass, and feel my heart break every hour on the hour. "Don't touch that dial! We'll be right back, but first, here's a slew of trash set to current music you don't need but apparently can't live without!" Fuck. My. Life.

You want to know why I'm still angry after all these years, after I've been able to leave all the nightmares and pain of my childhood on the battlefield? It's very simple: the world has cheapened EVERY FuckING THING I spent my life dreaming about doing, and *you* let it happen. You: the Great Consuming Leaches of the world. You: the easiest route between points A and B. You: the Global Sense of Entitlement and Expectancy. You: the Holder of the Keys and the Maker of Change. You have done this, all because it's so fucking easy. Your ability to make excuses to feel okay about it also seriously makes me want to fucking kill myself. You cast around for any way to condone your actions, and those rebuttals are as shallow as a puddle in a desert. You go online and look for people like yourself to help back you up, and it looks like a bunch of spoiled brats having a fit, throwing yourselves on the ground like irate toddlers who don't get a piece of candy. Face it: you steal music. You *steal* it. What's worse, I know why you steal it. Because 98 percent of the music out there today isn't worth buying.

There's the Catch 22. I sit here, indignant about how the state of the music union is, and I know damn well that if I were just another listener like you, I'd probably be stealing it too. Modern music is a joke. If it ain't Katy Perry swinging from a tree, caterwauling like a Kewpie Doll with breast implants, it's crap like what passes for "Active Rock Radio" today: a bunch of con artists and thieves "borrowing" from better songs and superior artists to create an amalgam of garbage so heinous, it's inestimable how it's been allowed to go on. But these thieves are smart because they know their audience. In other words, they know *you*. They know that you don't do your research or remember the past. They know that you don't pay for music, so why the fuck would you pay attention? They know that even if you put the original and the callous rip-off next to each other, with an expert pointing out all the similarities and places where they *blatantly* plagiarized the material, you don't care enough to be incensed about it, therefore letting these second-rate pukes get away with it. Good for you. It's no better than giving little kids awards for participating: how are we supposed to recognize excellence and exception when we're so busy rewarding mediocrity so as not to hurt people's feelings? Fuck the feelings—make me *feel something* other than disgust.

There is a rock album that came out in 2013 that is *so* derivative, it's impossible to describe it in one book. It's almost textbook: *every* song on that album is either a Metallica song, a Megadeth song, or an Iron Maiden song. The *real* metal fans know it and avoided the album like the plague. But the Metal by Numbers fans have no idea about the history of our genre, the great anthems that represent it, and the bands that made it vital in the first place. In other words, they don't know a fucking thing. So that band and others like them get away with musical murder. It's a shame, but it's true. Before you ask, no—I'm not going to tell you who it is. This is an example of me making you do your own legwork on the subject. Trust me when I say that when you figure it out, you'll be as disappointed as I was. What are they going to do, sue me? That means admitting that I'm right, and that'll never happen in this day and age. It also means giving up the anonymity I've allowed them here, safely tucked in these bleeding pages. So I guess we'll just see what happens. I didn't even mention the *other* band who does the same thing and in an even more flagrant fashion. One of their "hits" (I can't even say that without spitting on the ground) steals the melody line from Ozzy's song "The Ultimate Sin." It's right there for everyone to see. But no one sees it except, of course, for myself.

I hate it when I'm right.

On a humorous note, how fucking funny is it that Chad Kroeger married Avril Lavigne? I think that is the funniest shit I've heard in years, and that's saying something: Lemmy told me a filthy joke in a smoking lounge in Germany that involved grandmothers and fists, and that is a distant second place. Kroeger and Lavigne getting married makes weird sense on so many hilarious levels that if I think about it too long, I get an ice cream headache. But here's the issue that terrifies me: they are both made of the same matter, and if they touch each other too much they might fuck around and open a black hole here on Earth. Another thing that could happen is we could all go back in time or something. Let's just hope they cancel each other out peacefully—the last things we need are global time travel or a violent singularity in Toronto. Hopefully by the time this comes out, they'll have split up, saving us all from desecration. (Editor's note: THEY HAVE—that's a win in my book.)

One surprising by-product of the fact that so much modern music is Suck City is that I've gone back and discovered or redis-covered some old wonderful music I hadn't even thought to give a chance before. One genre in particular is jazz. Free, bebop, swing—it doesn't matter really: I've begun to envelope myself in this amazing exploration. The husky melancholy of Billie Holiday, the cerebral strike of John Coltrane, the massive moves of Sonny Rollins, Dizzy Gillespie and his brass acrobats, Dave Brubeck and his ocean jazz—there is *so* much to look into and enjoy that you never really know until you find it. Mind you, you need to have an ear for it to begin with. If you're a weekend warrior who only listens to Top Forty, I apologize, but there's a 99 percent chance you're not going to enjoy Miles Davis. However, if you dig you some adventure in the guise of risk and innovative improv, there's a hundred years of music to investigate. From Bix Beiderbecke to Thelonious Monk, you will not be disappointed.

I haven't mentioned Charlie Parker.

He and Dizzy Gillespie and a handful of others are really responsible for shaping the sound of modern jazz, and they did it way back in the 1940s. You listen to a recording like "Koko," and it has the same sense of incredible abandon that you get from early rock 'n' roll records or seventies punk songs. It was *that* explosive. It's insane to think it was recorded around 1945. But for all the moods and modes Parker had to offer, I have to be honest: it's a slow jam of his that I really enjoy the most. Some people choose to concentrate on his addictions and neuroses, but this one recording can silence them all.

"Lover Man," recorded in the late forties when Parker disappeared into the darkness of Los Angeles, might just be one of the saddest songs I've ever encountered. The sense of longing and regret you get from this tune makes you so pensive, I was on the verge of tears hearing it. I encourage everyone to listen to it—the live versions he did are good, but this studio session is the one you want to hear. Listen to it, then think about this when you do: it was one whole live take, recorded back before computers, and it sounds as good today as it did when it was released. After you put it in that perspective, you'll understand why modern music can sincerely suck my fucking dick.

Let's talk about the phenomenon known as EDM—electronic dance music. Now, I have no beef with these people or their music. I've seen the shit come and go: before EDM, there was techno. Before techno, there was rave. Before rave, there was electronica. Before electronica, there were DJs. I get it—I've seen it. It's nothing new and to each his own. But here's my fucking problem: they make huge amounts of money for live performances—*huge* amounts of money for live events. That Andy Samberg skit isn't just funny; it's damn near accurate. These "artists" make a lot of money for concerts. However, it's not really a concert, is it? It's really not, because essentially they turn up, plug their computer in . . . and push a button. That's what they do when they perform: they push a fucking button. That's because all their music is preprogrammed and set to go once they hit the stage. The person doesn't even need to turn up; they could just send their laptop along, and that would be it. They're not *doing anything.* That's why they wave their stupid arms around and jump and look like nuts. They don't do *anything.* Saying they are "performing" is a fucking LIE. That's what bothers me: real performers get onstage and bleed, giving it all they got. These DJs (I don't care whether that's not what they call them; that's what they fucking are) get up onstage, push *one button*, sit back, and make millions.

Fuck you.

That's an insult to every motherfucker who climbs on a stage and dies every night. That is an insult to all the musicians and bastards who've kept this industry from buckling for decades. Calling these shows "concerts" is as bad as saying George W. Bush was elected twice legally. I'm ashamed that people throw money at these DJs. A few of them actually create live, but the majority are a fucking *sham*. If they had a soul, they'd be awash in guilt. But they don't—they won't even care that I'm saying this. Joke's on them, though. Like I said, I've seen these trends come and go. I give them two years. Don't let the door hit you in your other face on the way out.

It ain't just music either, folks; it's the shows and movies on TV as well. There are shows so offensively idiotic that I almost exclusively watch puppet shows now at shopping malls around the world. There are days I don't even turn my TV on, and this is coming from a recovering Cable Junkie. I could sum the fucking mess that is modern garbage very simply. It'd only take two words. Drop your linen and commence to grinnin'. Here goes: *American Hoggers.*

I.

Give.

Up.

Every channel boasts of "hit" shows, then you see the commercials. They turn out to be just another fucking piece of trash in which a bunch of drunken rednecks party it up, fight and fuck, and quote bumper stickers like they're scripture and try a little too desperately to ignore the fact that they have absolutely no fucking future, that if they didn't have this show, they'd be digging ditches or turning tricks for those who dig ditches. They pretend that people in the world give a steamy shit about their fucking tawdry existence. They have to—the alternative is too fucking bleak to comprehend for them: that if they didn't exist, it wouldn't matter.

Wow, I'm bitter . . .

I'm so tired of "who's the best chef, artist, apprentice, house flipper, restaurant flipper, car flipper, snobby model, bad girl, rock whore, real housewife, nerd, *other* nerd, singer, voice, dancer, face, British talent, American talent, bachelor, bachelor-ette, storage locker buyer, tiny cheerleader, *fat* tiny cheerleader, survivor, celebrity survivor, big brother, big sister, rehab winner, weight loser, *different* weight loser, and amazing racer" shows that I've very nearly sold all of my televisions a hundred times in the last five years. I seriously thought these shows would be gone by now; instead, channels like Bravo would be out of business without them. It's disconcerting to a fault. The only things real about reality TV are the fucking headaches I get when I try to explain to someone that there are producers on the other side of the camera telling them what to do. Some people don't want to hear that shit. Some people are convinced that the chick with the rose and the spiky-haired dude who's always a little too sweaty are going to live happily ever after. Some people think that Honey Boo Boo is adorable and misunderstood, not horribly irritating and gross, which she is. To be fair, it's not just her—that whole family is a massive dose of diabetes with a GoPro. I'd rather fall asleep listening to recordings of farts from the 1920s than watch that fucking nightmare.

Maybe I wouldn't be such a prickish old bastard if the balance of stupid to smart weren't so out of whack. But almost everything on the telly is fucking drivel. If I have to stare at catty designers crying because their seams ripped out again, I'll carve up my nose to spite my face. You might be saying, "You don't *have* to watch those shows, Mr. Taylor." First of all . . . thank you, nobody calls me Mr. Taylor. But you can call me "Mad Beans" Hooper. Secondly, that's not *entirely* accurate, is it? Because it seems like every channel advertises on every *other* channel. I don't watch Bravo or HGTV or those other channels because I don't like those shows. But they *all* advertise on the channels I *do* watch, sticking all that silly horseshit in my face like a kid calling me a cocksucker from across the street, thinking that the rules don't apply because he's not on my property. That's fucking stacked up, pap. I don't give a shit about the next top model or top chef or top shot. The only "top" I want to bloody watch is *Top Gear.*

Swinging back to music while my blood's moving, I hinted earlier that modern music has the smell of used cat litter and tastes about as sweet. That's not fair—cat litter's just doing its job. Modern music has no excuse. People "write" this shit, record it, print it, send it out for consumption, and then proclaim enthusiastically that it's an "instant hit." I'd sincerely like to know how hits are made these days and who's writing them.

First of all, no radio station *really* plays your requests anymore. I've seen this firsthand: the DJs already have the next song dialed up and when you call and try to request something, they assure you that they might be playing it later, then because they're always recording the calls, they ask you whether you like "Blah-Blah-Blah." If you say yes, I like "Blah-Blah-Blah," they then cut that recording up so it sounds like you called and said, "Hey, can I hear 'Blah-Blah-Blah'?" You sure can, they say, it's actually coming up next! Meanwhile, the song you actually called for? They don't even have it in the station. That's what happens to the requests for new music: they get tossed in lieu of hearing fucking "Blah-Blah-Blah" for the billionth fucking time. That's why radio is going away and satellite is taking over. People like to wait to hear what's next commercial-free(ish) rather than feel like they're being ignored. Shit happens, and it always happens on WSHT, playing what *we* think you *want* to hear, even if you *don't!*

Now for that "who wrote it" question. I've heard that six to ten people can be known to write for the likes of Katy Perry, Rihanna, or Miley Cyrus. That's six to ten people sitting in a room, "brainstorming." That's three to five pairs of human beings putting their heads together, going, "We need to recycle some of our crappiest hooks so they appear relevant!" I may be wrong, but these *might* be the same six to ten people who write for *all* of these sawed-off, hack-star, self-important pieces of shit, and *that* might be why EVERY SHITTY FuckING POP SONG THAT HAS COME OUT IN THE LAST SIX YEARS ALL SOUNDS LIKE THE SAME FuckING SONG OVER AND OVER AND OVER AND OVER AND FuckING OVER OH MY GOD MY CAPS COME OFF SOMEONE HIT MY MEDIC-ALERT BUTTON THE DAMN CAPS COME OFF . . .

That's better. Thank you.

Look at the number of people it takes to come up with those songs, and they're not even in the band, if those tool bags have bands. It took six to ten people to write those songs? Are you kidding me? Guess what? I'm fairly certain Dave Grohl wrote "Everlong" by himself. I'm quite sure Ray Lamontagne wrote "Burn" by himself (although his newer stuff has gotten quite Coachella). I wrote "Through Glass" by myself. Freddie Mercury envisioned "Bohemian Rhapsody" on his own. Speaking from experience, I know there's a wonderful dynamic that comes from writing in a group. But that dynamic specifically comes from writing as a group who *plays* together, who performs together, who runs the risks together. That's how you write a song. That's how you find a hit. That's how you make real music . . . not crammed in someone's conference room spit-balling buzzwords you feel the kids will gravitate toward "especially in the summer!" I swear, man. It's enough to make me want to pull my own head off and kick it across the street.

This shit's real to me. This isn't funny anymore. Well, you may be laughing right *now*, but that's because sometimes I'm hilarious when my temper's up. That's as may be, but I'm still upset. You see, music used to be the only real thing there was out there to me. You had to be *good* at it to make it, or you had to at least *look* good sounding bad, which could be equally awesome. Now? It doesn't matter. People are predisposed to an amount of success before they even hit the street, depending on how much money the labels sink into you. There are no real homegrown heroes anymore. There aren't even any real overnight success stories anymore. Every unit is a calculation, and every release is a way to set up their next release. Everything in between is a fucking lie. Unless the Uppers have a monetary confidence in you, you could find yourself getting shelved in exchange for moving more backing for the next bout of One Direction pubescent crotch rot.

Honestly, I have to take that back. There's been one breakout sensation in the last five years that took the entire world by storm. Anybody who says they never hummed "Gangnam Style" is a motherfucking liar. Maybe it's just me, but it seemed like Psy came out of nowhere and, through the power of YouTube, basically made everyone look like fucking tossers. Maybe it's that fact that made me love that song . . . well, the first million times my son played it for me, anyway. After that, even I wanted that bastard to go away. But it *did* prove to me that the real spirit of musical discovery is still out there. YouTube and Spotify allow people to research the music without stealing it and robbing us tuneheads of careers. The Internet is the word on the street, the lights of the city, and the will of the people all blended together with pop-up porn and disabled cookies. Then again, until recently I had no idea who the fuck this Shawn Mendes kid is; now my niece and her friends won't shut up about him. It makes me want to take tiny puppies to get their ears pierced. Honestly, I don't know the kid, but if Beiber is any indication of what history has in store, I'm looking forward to hating his fucking guts in the future.

By the way . . .

Fall Out Boy Will Save Rock 'n' Roll.

Eat shit and fucking die, Fall Out Boy.

Folks, it's really the commercials that are killing me.

I curse and flip off my TV more now than when I did when I was younger. If I had a cane, I'd be whipping it through the air like a polo player on PBR. As of this writing, there is a commercial that haunts me, taunts me, and flaunts itself in my own house (the house I PAY THE BILLS for . . . sorry, totally in character there . . .). I get up in the morning, and as soon as I mash the buttons on the remote control, within minutes I am assaulted by the banal bullets of its condescension. I'm starting to hear the fucking thing in my dreams—I swear I woke up and I'd dug my nails into my palms. It's lower-case music for a higher clientele, seeing as weed is fast becoming fairly legal in this country. I get it: know your demographic, but holy mother of bastards, I hate it with a deep passion.

"S, apostrophe, M-O-R-E . . . S'more for you and S'more for me . . . "

Those lyrics make me want to kill penguins in front of children.

Dairy Queen has lost my business for *life* all because of that bearded hippie and his frickin' acoustic sing-along from hell. Not since "Kumbaya" and "The Hokey Pokey" has a song made my blood curdle and my veins scream for vengeance. I thought we'd crossed the threshold of common decency when the Honey Nut Cheerios bee started doing parodies of hip-hop songs ("Hey . . . Must be the *honey!*" Fuck my life . . .). But the hack in the DQ commercial that looks like a hipster lumberjack makes me ashamed to tell people I can play an acoustic guitar. The fact that there are children in that ad—CHILDREN, PEO-PLE! REAL, IMPRESSIONABLE CHILDREN!—makes me want to call DHS and report the director and all the people involved with R&D at that company for endangerment. Goddamnit, this is AMERICA! I want JUSTICE!

I really mean that. People in commercials should be chemically castrated.

Between Owl City and Carly Rae Jepsen making a song together that is so sugary sweet your teeth fall out when you listen to it too often and the propensity for well-established bands to abandon their edgy rock roots in favor of music that might sell to the dilapidated masses temporarily obsessed with dance elements, you'll understand my murderous rage at the moment. Things just aren't looking better. Things don't sound better. There are moments during the day when I have an uncontrollable urge to smash every instrument within arm's reach, like Bluto in a toga hopped up on hops, barley, and indignation. If the world's going to end someday, I was kind of hoping the soundtrack wouldn't suck so fucking bad. But when the melodies are electronically corrected and the humanity has been sucked clean, it makes me beg for the apocalypse. It's shit like this that makes me monitor my kids' listening habits. It's shit like this that makes me seriously consider early retirement.

But I have a better idea . . .

I'm going to start a new band.

We're going to be called the Buseys. It'll be me and four other people with huge necks. We're going to dress in flannel shirts, corduroy pants, and workman's boots. We're going to grow our beards out to ridiculous proportions and weave glittery beads into our eyebrows. When we play live, we'll wear helmets of all kinds: batting helmets, football helmets, motorcycle helmets—almost anything with a chinstrap. We'll all have mouthpieces like boxers, and we won't take them out for the entire show—we'll sing through them, we'll spit through them, we'll talk to the audience through them, and so forth. During songs we'll head-butt each other furiously. Every song will be pissed off punk rock, started with a nearly unintelligible "1–2–3–4–1–2–3–4!" When we go into the studio, we'll wear the helmets and use the mouthpieces. When we do photo shoots, we'll use the helmets and wear the mouthpieces. We won't sell T-shirts at our shows; we'll only sell (wait for it . . .) helmets and mouthpieces.

It'll be the most ludicrous idea the world has ever seen. But it's *just dumb enough* that the Buseys will end up conquering the entire music industry. Our "albums"—incoherent garbles of noise because we record with the mouthpieces and head-butt while we're tracking—will go triple-platinum in a world where the download is still king. Grammies will be laid at our doorsteps, mainly because the Grammy committees are too terrified to invite us to the ceremonies. We'll provide songs for Bond movies, Marvel movies, Transformer movies, Cameron Diaz movies . . . The world will be our oyster and we'll eat it with vinegar and salt. Just when we think we've gone as far as we possibly could go, we'll record a covers EP on the space station, play a "one-night-only" gig on the moon . . . then slip back into the shadows like nothing ever happened.

At least one of the Buseys will marry a Kardashian—we can't all be geniuses. Another will use his infamy to run for the US Senate. Still another will parlay the money he's made into a pyramid scheme aimed directly at rich people, aggravating the world economy with a savage burn on the upper 1 percent's infrastructure. One will die after a night spent doing tequila shots laced with blowfish poison. I will simply become a carney, pulling levers on rickety rides and challenging out-of-towners to "hit the bull's eye and win the big-ass stuffed animal, cocksucker!" I'll deny ever being in the band, and I'll take to wearing an eye patch to avoid any and all conversations about my "former

group." Then, in forty years, we'll do a Buseys reunion, and one
of us will have a stroke onstage in mid-head-butt during our hit
single "NNNHHHNNNMMMET." And that will mark the end
of an idea I strictly put together as a joke to protest shitty music.

Stranger things have happened.

Hollywood Undead started out as a fake hip-hop band. They're
huge now. SOD began as a one-off; now they're revered across the
metal landscape. If you think the Buseys couldn't take the world
by its scrotum and tear it off while screaming in its big dumb
face, you have no real clue as to what this planet finds fascinating
at times. From the Gorillas to Death Klok, sometimes crazy is
ingenious. Sometimes it takes something so left of center to kick
the culture right in its "pop." It doesn't matter whether the band
is a figment of someone's deranged imagination, not even human,
or literally two-dimensional; if the people get their energies out
for it, you can bet it'll be an overnight sensation. Just look at
Babymetal. If it weren't so cute and catchy, I'd be scared to death.

The fact of the matter is that it really doesn't matter whether
your music is shit (which it is). It simply doesn't matter whether the
artists you worship are fucking numb in the skull (which they
are). It doesn't matter that the people you put on pedestals—
musical, political, pop star, rock star, movie star, or otherwise—
aren't worth the prestige they're printed on most of the time
(ditto totes). Kill squads are capital, black bags bulging with secret
pockets perpetually empty . . . and all we're doing is humming
along, too distracted by the pretty colors to shut our eyes because
if we did, we'd realize none of the music is in tune or on key. We'd
realize our background noise is a fucking thunderous fart with a
funky beat. James Brown is rolling over in his grave, and he ain't
feeling good about it.

How do you explain to a kid that a band isn't one dude with a
laptop and an external aux cord? Where do you possibly begin

to try to fan out the facts for a child who has seen nothing but *Yo Gabba Gabba* and *Fresh Beat Bands* flailing around in major keys, singing about the most inane shit ever. Yes, yes, I know: nice melodies and simple messages help children learn to love music. And yet those responsible for the din start "real" bands, bands that are five fucking minutes old, with essentially the same children's garbage tunage, and they win a Grammy for Best Rock Album—that would be the band Fun again. That's just no fun at all.

My biggest fear is that this isn't a passing fad; it's just the beginning. Someday, when I'm even older than I am now (shut it . . .), I'll be putting on work slacks to go out and water my petunias in the afternoon when suddenly a car full of young ruffians will roll by, with windows tinted too dark and the bass pumped too loud, playing noise that is passing for popular exciting music. I'll listen for a second, and with my uncanny ability to pick shit apart at a moment's notice, I'll realize with real panic that what I'm hearing is several layers of auto-tuned farts, backed by a collage of tubas, mouth harps, and jazz guitars. When the farts aren't enough, 808s will blow the Brown Sound into my neighborhood with such violence that the people next door will spontaneously combust in an explosion of diarrhea and polyester pantsuits. As the crap rolls out of earshot, I'll lean against my Tempur-Pedic adjustable bed and stare out the window, wondering what in the sheer silky fuck has happened to the population's hearing. I'll put on my cowhide gloves, head into the garden, and begin my work, only to find myself humming that fart song without even knowing it. The lesson here is simple: catchy is catchy, but there's still no accounting for taste. It's always the songs you hate the most that get stuck in your head all the damn time, which sucks because the only way to get it out is to listen to it, and that ain't fucking happening. You just have to grit your teeth and get through it.

Music, TV, movies, Internet, books (those are what you download on your Kindle Fires, kids)—everywhere you look it's like entertainment is falling down under the weight of its own trash. I'll paraphrase Michael Bay, who summed it up best when he told his critics he didn't give a shit what they thought of his latest *Transformers* installment because, "You're all going to see it anyway." He was right; it was the first film of 2014 to cross the $100 million mark in its first weekend in the United States. Bay could keep making these fucking flicks until he has his body frozen to outlive the future. It won't make any difference. The lemmings are going to head for the cliff with nothing on their minds other than feeling the whoosh of the wind cross their fuzzy faces as they plummet toward the canyon floor. That's us: we're the lemmings. Depending on how you look at it, our sense of entertainment is either the wind in our faces or the ground pushing our faces back through our skulls. Either way, we're really fucked.

The saying used to be "Shit happens." I added to it in my own way: "Shit happens—just don't let it happen all over you." Now, with the way of the world and the world in the way, it's time for a new saying: "SHIT SELLS." That's right: you all love your shit. From your derivative music to your shiny hollow movies, from those videos displaying your idiocy on the Internet to your addiction to fake reality on TV, that saying is a fucking fact. Shit sells, and it sells really well. That's because the people slinging that shit around know their audience. They know that you'll buy, watch, and listen to shit if it's shiny enough. They all think you're dumb, and it doesn't bother them in the slightest. They will suck content and intelligence out of their products happily, keeping the costs low, so they can get a deeper yield from their product. That's all it is: product. No art, no heart, no goals, and no soul. Just straight, unadulterated garbage for your pleasure. If I were you, I'd be insulted. I'm not insulted because I don't buy their shit. I boycott it.

You want to feel better about yourselves? You want to prove that you're all not eating shit? Then grab a placard, stand your ground, and boycott as well. Make a statement that has nothing to do with voting for some shit-kicker on *The Voice*. Choose carefully when looking for movies—don't just rush into the latest YA (that's "young adult," parents) movie that sucks so hard the actors all have Lemon Face. Avoid crotch-shot vids and YOLO comps on YouTube, Vine, Insta-crap. Feed your brain something other than vacuous chaos and mediocre drivel. Challenge yourself to read a book with no pictures in it. Find a show that has some substance that might actually make you think. Listen to some music that doesn't just repeat the word "Baby" 23,457 times. Your brain and intellect—these things are a lot like your body. If you feed it well, it blossoms and grows and gets stronger. If you feed it nothing but empty fast food calories, you're gonna find yourself breathing through your mouth and dragging your knuckles on concrete as you make your way to the unemployment office.

Ask yourself this: after we've killed each other off or reached a point in our technology at which we can leave this planet and populate the universe with our nonsense, when the aliens come to sift through the wreckage of our civilization in the aeons to come, what do you want them to find? Do you want them to judge us by Bach or Bieber? Do you want them to read Victor Hugo or *The View's Summer Cookbook*? Do you think they'll assume the greatest of us all was Stephen Hawking or Johnny Manziel? Based on what they find, will they come to hunt us down so we can't spread our buffoonery across the cosmos? Or will they simply look around at all the garbage left behind, contemplating the shit we used to distract ourselves with, scratch their tentacles, look at each other, and say, "Really? *This* is what they thought was good?"

Yes, I worry about what the aliens will think of us. I'm no "ancient astronaut theorist." I don't think we've been visited by a more advanced species. I don't think they're plotting to come invade. I think that if they're watching, they're doing the same thing I am: wondering why the fuck you people are mesmerized by all of this half-assed entertainment. They're sitting in their spaceships, watching our habits, and they've come to the conclusion that we're all apes in designer clothes. They think we're fucking dumbasses. They are amazed that we can feed and shelter ourselves with all the stupidity we involve ourselves with. Worse yet, they believe our stupidity is contagious. They think that if they come here to make contact, they might catch our "dummy" virus. It scares the living . . . well, whatever they call their poop, that's what gets scared out of them. And these amazing beings, beings beyond our capacity to understand, are leaving us alone. They have quarantined themselves from us. They ain't coming back until the house is empty and the lights are all off, and only then will they wait to see whether there's still any "stupid" blowing around in the wind. They're keeping their distance, which is a disappointment to me. That's because I really wish they'd come back to pick me up and take me with them. With all the brain damage in the world today, you can't blame me.

The world's IQ is approaching single digits. The looks in people's eyes are glassy and glossy, staring past the person next to them and out into the distance at nothing in particular. The bastard thing about it is that I'm getting too tired to fight it.

Who will help me?

Chapter 10

Hello, Pot—I'm Kettle

I'd like to use this opportunity and platform to fill in the blanks about some unknown facts regarding the handsome author of the book you hold in your hands. That would be me, if anyone was wondering. Cheeky bastards—you try to slip one nice thing about yourself onto paper, and they pounce on it like a rat on nipples . . .

Let me just set the record straight: I have never knowingly eaten my own boogers. That might be contrary to popular belief but it's true—they were all by accident, and let me say, I didn't enjoy them. Seriously! A few have indeed made their way into my mouth via running or vigorous sweat rotation. However, I've never done anything to hasten their descent, like tilting back for easier access. Having read that last sentence, I can honestly say that could be taken a lot of different ways, and I'm embarrassed to have written it. Then again, as you can see I haven't deleted it, so I must not give a runny-thong stain whether anyone cares—either that, or I need the word count. It's getting harder and harder to space these fucking books out to the appropriate length. So just to sum up: I have never eaten my nose resin of my own volition, but in certain circumstances I have come to know (and appreciate) the taste and color. I'm not sure what bearing that has on what we're here to discuss, really, but the point, I guess, is to show that I am no Zeus lording over the council; I am just as horribly fucked up as you are.

I have a long-standing relationship with idiocy. We go way back. We're "totes close," as people who will outlive me might say. However, I am not oblivious to its existence like some folks are. I am well aware that I have blank patches in the rearview image of my mind, sort of like the blind spots where you can't see the other cars or, in this case, the places where your intelligence touches cotton just before the know-how takes a shit. Think about those moments when you're just about to do something, probably something you've done a million times, and suddenly your brain plays a game of Files Not Found. You find yourself standing in the middle of the kitchen, wondering why in the sheer fuck did you wander in there in the first place. Until you reboot, that's exactly where you stay, twisting a bit with a quizzical look that conveys to everyone who sees it that you are confused and need an adult. That happens to me a lot. Welcome to the Hell of Duh.

The Hell of Duh is a fixed point on a moving moment: it is able to cut across every single smart thing you have ever done and make you feel like a moron who still needs supervision. Every man, woman, and child through history, from Gandhi to Gulliver in his travels, has had to dance at the barrage of bullets called the Hell of Duh, prancing to avoid getting shot in the toes. We are just as prone to Kemp as we are to Kemper—such is life as a slack-jawed human looking for sustenance and satisfaction.

I am no stranger to these proclivities; as smart as I purport to be, I am just as much a fuck-up as I am a purveyor of frivolous writ. We all have a golf bag full of crosses to bear. Mine resemble the rakes I'm too stupid to walk around in the yard, ensuring that the big wooden handle smacks me right in the fucking face. It's been a problem as long as I can remember . . . in fact, let me tell you about the time I shot a hole in my grandmother's wall and blamed it on an unfortunate vacuum cleaner accident.

Every word of that sentence is true: I'll explain . . .

I must have been twelve years old. My sister Barbi and I were in Des Moines for the summer, staying with my Gram and hanging out with our cousins from Indianola. It was the day after a sleepover at Gram's house. We'd spent most of the time at the cousins' house, so we gave my Aunt Sandy a break and went to Des Moines. It was my cousins Craig and Todd, my sister, and myself alone in my Gram's house while she was at work. Now, I'm on record about my Gram being something of a collector—not a hoarder, just too stubborn to let go of anything. This means her house is a bit of a treasure trove, full of wonders from every decade and the various generations who lived there. To a group of young kids with nothing to do, it's basically an open-season challenge to see what you can find. Everything from artifacts from the sixties to fancy dice brought home from Vegas were up for grabs. So the scavenger hunt was on.

We fanned out around the house, intent on discovery and a tiny pinch of mischief. My Gram's house is a fairly simple format: through the front door is the living room. Heading to the left takes you to the kitchen, with access to the garage (to the left) and the basement (down the stairs to the right) through their respective doors. If you turned right through the living room, you gained egress to the bedrooms and the bathroom, all built around a tiny hallway that separates them. You could literally leave one bedroom, take a step, and be in another bedroom—it was close quarters living, but it was and still is a very nice house that I enjoyed living in. Until I bought my own houses, my Gram's place was the longest I ever lived in one spot, and to this day I still consider that the house I grew up in.

Anyway, Craig went into the garage. Barbo, as I called her, was in a spare bedroom. Todd was in the living room. I was in the spare bedroom closest to the living room, digging about. It was the room that had the most dressers and drawers in it, so I'd called dibs on it. One time I'd found an entire "Paint by Numbers" set in there. Upon completion I saw that it was a very sardonic representation of a clown woman, brown hair flowing back behind her head and white face paint running into her lipstick. Then again, that might have been because I'm terrible at painting or drawing, but to *me*, it was an unusually stirring example of the eternal struggle between happiness and misery. It was the best thing I'd ever attempted to claim as illustrative art.

My cat named Scratch pissed on it. It was thrown away. Long story . . .

So back to why I'm rambling in your puffy earlobes right now: the gang of family and I were nosing around the "catacombs" of the original Chez Taylor. While my familial colleagues were busy elsewhere, I was in a room full of wonderment, examining everything within or without arm's reach. I looked up at the wall . . . and that's when my eyes fixed on my Uncle Alan's old .30-06, which for those not in the know is basically a shotgun.

A thought occurred to me . . .

Dudes and chicks, listen: I was twelve. I already didn't know shit from shit. I could barely find my penis on a map, let alone discern a good idea from a bad decision. So let me describe the carnage that ensued with what can only be called "journalistic integrity"—meaning I won't sugarcoat my Hellish Duh for the benefit of the cameras and those watching at home. It's quite simple: I wanted to hold the damn thing in my hands like a hunter. Any time this idea had come to me in the past, my Gram had always been there to thwart my stupidity. But now I was on my own, left to devices that were most likely running low on power. So with no one to stop me, I reached up and took the gun from its vaunted place on the rack, cradled it in my hands, and waved it around a bit. It was heavy—American steel and wood comingling in a classic fashion designed to make bad things disappear and living animals turn into dinner. Having that thing in my hands should have registered as a responsibility, not as a toy. But again, I was twelve—literally every idea I'd had up to that point was terrible. But none of them were as bad as the one I was about to make in that moment.

I pulled the trigger.

That's how I found out it'd been loaded.

Why the hell was the thing loaded? I was twelve: I didn't know that you always check to make sure that a gun isn't loaded before you do anything with it. I didn't know that it was an even bigger mistake to pull the trigger on a strange gun in an enclosed space. So you can imagine what happened next. The gun went off, blowing a hole in the bedroom wall and filling the room with noise and smoke. It was *extremely* loud. I didn't hear myself scream bloody murder because it had scared the ever livin' fuck out of me. I didn't hear a lot of anything because my ears were ringing like the morning after they choose a new pope. I missed the cries of surprise from the other rooms from my sister and Craig, who I had also scared to death. But the real panic set in when I realized that the wall I'd just shot through faced the living room. Todd had been in the living room. I froze. Suddenly this wasn't just a mistake; this was turning into a fucking nightmare.

Two things were going for me that day: (1) luck decided to move Todd over a couple of feet just before I'd fired the gun, and (2) the gun had been loaded with weak buckshot, not a slug. So after the initial explosion from the gun and even though it had punched a hole through the wall, the energy was dispersed enough that it merely sent a spray of BBs across the living room. I think one hit Todd, but it was harmless. A few, however, did chip the TV screen a bit, and the carpet was littered with tiny metal balls and drywall. So as I was being screamed at by my family for nearly killing my cousin (I *said* I was sorry, but you know . . .), I pulled out Gram's ancient-ass vacuum cleaner. It was one of the old ones you drug behind you, with a long hose that connected to a long metal tube that *then* connected to the sucking mechanism. It was a classic POS: tape had been used to keep the metal tube connected to the sucker because it was always coming apart, and the body of the vacuum was so heavy that you needed two hands to drag the fucker anywhere. It was while I was cleaning up the debris that I hatched an ingenious plan.

The hole in the wall was very visible from the living room; you could see the bedroom through it. But there was a closet door that swung open and obscured the light flooding through it. So I stuck a rag in the hole on the bedroom side and opened the closet door to hide the evidence—nobody was going to open or close it to get a better look if they didn't know what to look for. By putting the rag in the hole, from the living room side it just looked like a hole in the wall, not the scene of a crime. I told my cousins and my sister my plan and threatened them with silent violence if they didn't toe the line. When Gram came home, she totally knew that something had happened; she just didn't know what. That's when I explained to her that "as I was vacuuming the hallway, that damn metal tube had come unhooked from the tube. The slip threw me off balance, and all my weight fell on the metal tube, which *then* punched a hole in the wall of the living room." She listened dutifully, nodding a bit and studying the hole. Because the rag was in the hole on the other side, it appeared that it was only on the living room side. With a pinch of skepticism, she bought it. At least she said she did. I'm fairly certain you could still smell the gunpowder and there was still a bit of plaster on the floor. But she said she believed me.

My cousins and Barbo couldn't believe it. Todd didn't speak to me for a while.

Obviously I'm not twelve anymore. I've gotten older, but I haven't gotten any better. You know what it is? I'm great at the big shit and the trivial shit but I suck at the little things. Well, they may not seem little to anyone else, but that's how I look at them anyway. Cook a big dinner for the whole family? No sweat—I'm your man. But ask me to program a garage-door opener? Nope—I'm as lost as a remote in the couch cushions. Mow the lawn, call some shots, or wax eloquently about the Battle of Hastings in 1066? Gimme the ball skipper and I'll take it to the hole. Adjust the settings in the car, change out the filter in the furnace or AC unit, or deal with some shit at the Department of Motor Vehicles? I might as well be ten years old with a bus ticket: I don't know what to do, where I'm going, or who to meet when I get there. I know to some of you this shit is pretty simple. To me, it's like trying to work calculus with a hacky sack. I've made peace with the fact that I'm great at some shit and rubbish at others. But it took patience and about twenty years to figure it out.

If I'm being completely honest, most of my profound ignorance seems to circle around any dealings I have with money. It's the biggest reason I have a very powerful man I only quietly refer to as "Mr. Shore" handling these things for me—and God help me, if I don't call him "Mr. Shore." He has a paddle in his office with my name branded into the wood. Money is a motherfucker if you don't know how to handle it. I've mentioned some of my bigger financial missteps in *Seven Deadly Sins*. But those are just the whales. My pond still has a few quirky fish swimming in it. I once paid $100 to a guy selling speakers out of the back of a van. I received one speaker that I then had to drag home, only to find out from Economaki that it wasn't worth a shit. One time I traded my old drum set for a guitar worth half as much. Can you see the trend here? I'm not great with "worth," really. As recently as a year and a half ago I decided I was going to get tickets for my family and I to attend a Daniel Tosh concert in Las Vegas. Feeling like a real adult, I went online, found a site that was selling tickets, and bought enough for all of us. I didn't look at other sites and I didn't compare prices to see whether I could find them cheaper; I just hit "Buy Now." You can imagine my embarrassment when I was shown I'd paid about four times too much for these seats. My defense? "But they're second row!" It didn't help my case.

If I had a defining story for how abysmal I am with money, it would be the Overpriced Rickshaw Story.

Now to the people who inhabit New York City and any other metropolis that is infested with these modes of transportation, you know what a rickshaw is. Anyone who has watched more than twenty-six episodes of *Seinfeld* may remember Kramer's gambit with his own rickshaw and the ensuing rigmarole. But for those who don't know, a rickshaw is basically a bike connected to the backseat of a car, usually with a canopy of some sort to shield the passengers from the sun. The originals were more like carts, with the controller pulling it along by its two long handles like a running back training in the off season. But the modern rickshaw looks like it has more in common with Lance Armstrong than Forrest Gump, and you don't need dope or new blood to tool along the mean streets of that city. They feel a little rugged when they first cast off, but once they get a head of steam going, they fly like a bomber on a night raid and inflict about as much damage on the flow of cars and trucks as well as your spine. Now you can visualize what a rickshaw is. So now my tale can begin . . .

A few years ago Steph and I had brought the kids out on the Mayhem Tour with us: Griff, my niece Haven, and my nephew Drew along with my sister-in-law Jackie and our family friend Kira. We were lucky enough to have a couple of days off in New York City, so we all went on a family sightseeing adventure. Ironically the day would be capped off by dinner with Mr. Shore and his lovely wife. When it was time to head to the restaurant, we discovered there were a few too many of us to get in one cab. No big deal: there are cabs all over the island. But I had a better idea, and by "better" I really mean "a terrible idea that started out as an innocent way to have fun." Don't all terrible ideas start out that way? I'm sure when Napoleon invaded Russia, he was thinking, "Christmas will be great! Snow and vodka for EVERYONE!"

I've been coming to NYC for years now, and in all that time I would watch the men and women ripping around on the rickshaws with a subtle sort of fascination. They always had people onboard, they were always moving as fast as their legs would scramble, and they were always engaged in what appeared to be daredevil stunt work, crossing against traffic and flying through intersections like hybrid demons hell-bent on getting to their destination. In all my time going to the city I'd never taken the opportunity to get in one, to taste that speed and insanity for myself. At that moment, standing there trying to get my family from point A to point B, I decided the time for waiting was over, and I was dragging the people I love with me. I flagged down two of these hellions, loaded up my brood, and, with a smile, we headed deep into New York rush hour. I should have known it was too good to be frugal.

The ride itself was a blast. We were shooting gaps and running reds all the way across town. My kids were losing their minds. Steph was laughing her ass off. Even though I was sweating through my clothes, I was really enjoying it. Griff's eyes looked like they were going to pop out of his head. Our bike-riding freelancer was peddling his ass off, dodging fenders and bumpers with no real thought to our safety. But it didn't matter—it was exhilarating, invigorating, and fascinating. You can't see the depths of the ocean in anything but a submarine; there's no way to get out and experience that world without a bunch of protective gear on. But being in that rickshaw, doing some serious human-powered speeds, it was the closest you could ever get to experiencing traffic without a car, like you were flying through the streets with none of the protection that the backseats or front seats afford you. It was like a ride at Disneyland. "You've flown over California—now DRIVE THROUGH NEW YORK WITHOUT BEING ENCLOSED IN A CAR!" It was an astonishing ride.

The bottom fell out of our boat when we reached the restaurant.

I'd hired two of these rickshaws, three of us in each rig. I didn't know there was a pricing list on the side of the basket with a ridiculous breakdown of each charge. There was a charge for each person . . . fair enough—cabs are like that too. But it was a *full* charge for each person, not just a percentage like it is in the taxis. Then it just got fucking stupid. Every mile was a different charge. Riding on a street was a different charge. Riding on an *avenue* was different charge. Riding on a *boulevard* was a different charge. It may be the anger with which I'm remembering this shit, but I'm almost certain that a left turn was more expensive than a right turn. So, all in, a two-and-a-half-mile trip for six people in two rickshaws, something that might have cost a miniscule amount in a regular cab . . . cost me $300. As rad as that ride was, I find it extremely difficult to find a way to justify that price. I've had cheaper plane tickets. But because I didn't ask how much it would cost, because I didn't know to look on the damn thing for a price list, because the guy was arguing with me that it was my own fault for not knowing what I was getting into, I swallowed my pride and paid the price. I've said before that the hardest lessons are usually the best because the pain gives you memory and you can't erase that kind of knowledge. All I can say is my family loved the ride, my wife didn't kill me for how expensive it was, and that rickshaw driver is fucking lucky I wasn't carrying my Louisville Slugger with me.

I didn't tell Mr. Shore about the incident. I won't send him a copy of this book.

Please don't send him one, because he scares me.

I've spent the better part of my life trying to figure out why my brain works the way it does. I'm no scrub, man: I can do my own laundry (sorta) and change the oil in my own car (not very well, but you get the idea). I can handle bigger pictures a little better than the smaller snapshots. It's fucking frustrating, not just to me but also to my family. Occasionally my wife will ask me to perform some menial task, and I'll feel a look cross my face like a shadow on a stone in the Mojave Desert. I know it's a visible change too because my wife *sees* it happen, looks at me, and says, "You don't know what I'm talking about, do you?" In the past I used to sputter and puff up like it was a strategic blow to my manhood. Now I just shrug and say, "nope." As you get older a funny thing happens: you stop giving a shit. It's awesome, really. I don't give a fuck anymore about what I wear, where I'm going, or whether anyone cares about it. It's wonderful rein-forcement for an ego that has spent a few too many times in the gladiator's circle, picking bits of sand and blood out of his eyes.

I think it's because of the way I grew up. I'm not going to harp on the suck-fest or regurgitate the abuse; I've documented that in other tomes. This is more about the effect than the cause. Because of the way I grew up, I had to learn how to do every-thing on my own. I had no father present to point me in any direction, and because the whole parental unit in general was spread pretty thin, I had to do things my way—that is, the hard way. I learned to cook, clean, drive, work, love, live, spend, hate, fight, run, smoke, think, fail, win, fuck, and regulate on my own. I was basically surrounded by a horde of adults who had no fucking clue how to keep their shit together. So it was a mat-ter of survival: I either had to figure it out or crumble under the weight of my own psychoses and shortcomings. Neither of those choices was very appealing, but I'd be damned if I was going to fail. So I did shit the hard way or came up with short-cuts that did more disaster than good. In the winters I would go out and clear all the snow off of my Gram's car. Because I'm a little short, I used a broom to reach the stuff on the roof and whatnot. It got to the point at which I was using it on the whole car because it was faster, fairly efficient, and I could get in out of the cold quicker. It wasn't until the summer that I realized by using a broom I was scratching the holy hell out of the paint on my Gram's car. What's more, it was *very* noticeable. She was, suffice it to say, very displeased with me. That's just a tiny taste of the consequences involved in developing your own thought process.

It's not necessarily a bad thing. I have a habit of thinking outside the box and the norm, which is probably why I write and act the way I do or come up with the different stories I like to imagine. It's taken me around the planet several times, allowed me to publish a few books and grow a moustache for a movie role, and, essentially, let me get away with proverbial murder with my friends. But they never let me forget that quite a few of my wires are crossed and mislabeled. Hey, what are you gonna do? When I wasn't in a trailer, I grew up on the road. Normal isn't exactly in my fucking wheelhouse when it comes to practicality or reality. Besides, I can smoke through my belly button. What can all of *you* do, fuckers and truckers?

Then there's the scary shit. Have you ever been sitting somewhere by yourself . . . and you suddenly realize you've been staring into space for like an hour? Oh, and the spot you were peering into? Someone is now sitting or standing there—you didn't even notice they'd taken up residence, but now they're staring right back at you, convinced you are the village rapist, waiting to toss them in your raper van and make off to the rape cave. By the time you come to from this incredible stupor, that person has made the rounds and told everyone in the area that you plan to probe them all. Before you can move, they're inching toward you ominously, pulling mace and perfume bottles out of massive purses, determined to recreate a scene from the classic movie *M*—and guess who they've picked to be Peter Lorre? Lesson being? A person can be obstinate, but a crowd can be made up of cock-sucking bastards.

They ruined my best Cramps T-shirt too . . .

Where was I going? . . .

See? It's *that* shit, right there. My tangents run further than Usain Bolt on a fat line of crank cut liberally with rocket fuel. What in the actual Fuck?! I know sometimes it's fun to follow a thought to the end of a trail, but Judas Priest on stage at Wembley, where does it *end*? Should I have cause for alarm? Should I consult a physician or at least David Copperfield? Before you say, "Why not Criss Angel?" . . . DON'T. Let it be known that I'll touch you with a dead man's pinky toe if you mention that guy's name. Criss Angel looks like Don Knotts auditioning for the role of The Crow. GODDAMNIT, I FuckING DID IT AGAIN! I'm going to go smoke—it helps me focus (and take a shit—DAMNIT! AGAIN!). I'll be right back.

Fifteen minutes and two Marlboro Golds later . . .

I still got nothin'. But now I'm light-headed and my knuckles smell like Dean Martin's nut sack. Yay team. Go me . . .

It's got to be the coffee. I was never this bad on cocaine. Besides the aforementioned cigarettes, coffee is my last real vice. I've cut out junk/fast food, I don't eat like a sixteen-year-old anymore, and I work out enough to keep the energy up and the love handles at bay. But the coffee makes me into a sweaty maniac standing around, assessing any situation with my hands on my hips, breathing like I just did a marathon at a sprint and not really sure how I ended up standing there in the first place. Caffeine is one thing; coffee is still another. I don't act like this when I have the rare soda or aberrant box of cookies. That just leaves the java as the culprit. Coffee is the rabid satanic blood that pushes my brain into the pillow and gets me to squeal. Knock it off, you suggest? Go fuck yourself, I reply. I'd rather be manic than mediocre. So why am I complaining? I'm not really sure. Sometimes I just wish I could concentrate while I'm hyper-crushing.

That's the name of the game: concentration. I have it on good authority that I have very little to no concentration whatsoever. The sad thing is that I know I passed this curse onto my son, Griffin. For you people who can do it, how the *fuck* do you people do it? I've missed entire scenes in movies before because a bug flew in my face. I get cruising down a rabbit hole, and by the time I reach the surface again, I'm in China. I know you can't dig a hole to China, but metaphorically speaking, that's what I mean. Don't argue with me in the middle of my book. It's *my book*! If I want to use an allegory that has been completely disproven in the modern day and age, I can! It's artistic license, and I didn't have to go to the local DMV to get it! I was born with it! Maybe *she* was born with it. Maybe it's Maybelline. The flash flood warnings are going off like crazy because I just rode the wave of confusion straight to the river again, and I'm screaming like a banshee on steroids. You want to try your hand at something fucking insane and agitated? Take a shot at living in *my* head for an hour or two. If you can make it fifteen minutes, I'll buy you a fucking Slurpee.

There are a few things I'm proud of, intelligently speaking. I've never used the term "YOLO" seriously. Whenever I hear someone say that and mean it, my skin crawls and I get very stabby. Also, I have *never* seen the movie *Titanic*. *Ever.* This drives my family and friends crazy because it's not that I'm against the saccharine take on an epic catastrophe (which doesn't make sense because *Titanic* is studied as a classic, but *Pearl Harbor* is vilified for basically the same reason). It's not because I have anything against anyone in the movie—I happen to think Leo DiCaprio and Kate Winslet are both fine, fine actors. It's not even about that fucking song by that fucking woman Celine Dion. No, I have a very credible (read by my family: asinine) reason for never seeing one of the biggest motion pictures of all time. It all came down to a radio interview back in 1997.

Back in '97 I was running the counter at the smut hut known as the Adult Emporium, slinging porn like Buffalo Bill Cody in a smock. Working by myself from midnight to 8 a.m., I tended to listen to a lot of radio at night, whistling along to oldies while I dusted racks and organized videos. I remember one night, as I was spraying Windex on some glass shelves to wipe away grime that might be distracting from the liquid latex and oil-based lubes, the DJ started talking about a recent interview in which James Cameron said, "By 1998, everyone in the world will have seen *Titanic!*"

Well, color me a stubborn asshole, but that sounded like a challenge.

I can remember thinking, "Where in the fuck do you get the gall to assume that? Why would you make a sweeping statement and decide that *this* movie—a tepid love story with a sinking toward the end—would be the movie that everyone would eventually see? How *dare* you assume that you know the tastes and fashions of an entire *planet* full of different people, all so you can make a mint on it!" I made up my mind that night that I would *never* see that movie, and I have held steadfast ever since. If it comes on TV, I change the channel. If my family wants to watch it, I leave the room. I know enough about the film's story through word of mouth and parodies that I'm not missing a fucking thing. Jack freezes and Rose blows a whistle, gets old, and dies in her sleep. The End: Yeah Bertha. I've read deeper brochures. The fact that this movie represents a high watermark for Billy Zane makes me angry at people for not putting him in more movies—he's *better* than that shit! Fuck!

My family kind of hates me for never seeing *Titanic*.

I've learned to live with it.

Let's wrap this pity party up real quick. Over the years I've done some dumb shit. I've disappeared into the heart of Amsterdam only to wake up in my hotel room, unsure of how I got there. To my count, I've asked seventeen different women how far along in their pregnancy they were . . . only to find out they were just fat. I've snorted pepper. I've smoked PCP. I waited in line for four hours to see *The Phantom Menace*. I've let myself get locked out of my own house completely naked (Thank God it was 2 a.m. and dark out). I've jumped through a glass coffee table wearing a helmet and a tutu in front of a living room full of people. However, I think the worst thing I've ever done is distrust my instincts. Now that I'm older, I tend to trust them more, but when I was younger, that wasn't the case. Here's an example.

I had a friend we'll call Bruce who was a bit of a freak. He was funnier than hell, and I really enjoyed hanging out with him. Other people had issues with him, but I would defend him and say, "He's just weird man—he's not a dick!" Nobody bought it, so it was usually just us, doing our thing and not giving a shit. One night long ago I was hanging at his house for the night when he jumped on the phone with some chick he wanted to hook up with. Before I knew it, he was telling me, "Grab your shoes— her parents aren't home, and she wants us to come over!" It was while I was wondering just how old this girl was that it occurred to me that this might not be such a great idea. But being a loyal friend, we left his pad and walked the couple of miles to her house. She let us in, and I felt very third-wheel-ish as they sat in her room smooching and chatting. So I went down to her living room to find something on TV.

I was right in the middle of *The Godfather* when her fucking parents came home.

I scrambled back up the stairs and yelled about their arrival, upon which the girl shoved us both into her closet to hide. I'll be honest: I was not stoked about the turn the evening had taken. Eventually her mother came in to say good night. There was a long pause. Finally her mother said, "Have you been smoking?"

The girl stammered, "N-No! Of course not!"

"Well, it smells like smoke in here!"

"Oh! I had my window open earlier—it probably came in then!"

I'll give her this—she was good. Her mother left.

We stood in that closet for another fifteen minutes before I said, "Fuck this. We're leaving." We left the closet, he said a quick good-bye to Jail Bait or whatever her name was, and we crept toward the stairs. The only way out was the front door, and her father was sitting exactly where I had been not twenty minutes ago, watching *The Godfather*. I looked at Bruce and said, "Follow my lead."

We went down the stairs.

I started gesturing at the ceiling and walls, speaking loudly. "Well, there doesn't seem to be any damage to the walls here, maybe we'll have to check outside—you see the *grading* is the problem . . . " Bruce picked it up and started spewing bullshit as well: "Yeah, that groundwater is definitely an issue, especially with how wet this summer has been . . . " We were nearly to the door—her father was sitting up, staring at us, mouth hanging open just enough to let us know he was stunned. I shouted back up the stairs, "HAROLD! Grab that socket wrench and meet us outside!" I grabbed the door handle, threw it open, hit the screen door, and shoved it wide, and just as her father was up and off the couch, we were out, sprinting down the street like madmen, laughing our balls off and praying to God that he wasn't dialing 911 at that very instant. Thank fuck this was over twenty years ago: he would have had his cell phone in hand calling for the authorities before we would have reached the bottom of the staircase. It was a funny end to an extremely stressful night.

But as the years wore on, Bruce became more and more erratic, and I began to see what everyone was on about. Then one day we just stopped hanging out. The last time I heard anything about him he had been in some trouble with some bad people. As much as I wanted to help him, I knew it wouldn't do any good. You see, by then I'd gotten a better read on my instincts. I'd learned the hard way that sometimes that feeling in your stomach is there for a reason. If you get that feeling and you ignore it, guess what? It's your fault when you get fucked over. If you come to learn from it, you can do wonders with it.

You see before you the ramblings of a man who knows just how ludicrous his musings are. It took a lot of trial and error to realize I am not the most brilliant bulb on the shelf. Yeah sure—I know it's been a long ride. But you don't make it to forty-one years old without (a) learning a few things that'll get you there and (b) figuring out you didn't know as much as you thought you did along the way. This is the beauty of being a part of your own life. Some people are quite happy just going with the flow and never ruffling any of the feathers on the bird of paradise. That's the right way to miss out on what life has to offer.

You've got to make some mistakes. You've got to admit early on that there's a good chance you know fuck all. It's okay to be a jackass; the problem comes when you never rise above that particular station.

I'm proud of my idiocy. It may have held me back from doing a few things. It may still be keeping me from winning any awards for exceptional intelligence. But I'll be okay. I may be stubborn, but at least I'm honest. Mensa isn't blowing my phone up; however, I can cook milk without burning it, and I don't leave bleach marks on my clothes when I do laundry. My wife still allows me to drive unattended and stay home with the kids, trusting that when she gets back they will not be singed, hungry, or dead. That's life as a man. That's life as a dad. That's life as the owner of an unusual mind. That works for me.

So I may have spent this entire book angry with you lot. I may have come right up to the cusp of my vocabulary and nearly gone over the edge because I get so infuriated with you that my eyes bulge like a puffer fish. I may descend into depressions in lieu of the fact that most of you shouldn't be alive, going the way of all the Darwin Award winners before you. That being said, just remember one thing as I rant in your direction: I'm no better than you. I may be more handsome and saucy, and I may be more verbally dexterous from time to time. But I didn't learn to lift the seat and put it back when doing "my number-one business" until a few years ago. I'm just as much of a scrub as everybody else. But I can be taught. I can be trained. I may even kind of like it in a weird, dirty way. So whereas my software only needs some subtle backing up once in a while, the rest of you may be fucked for all time. It's cool, though. If you're like me, feel good about the fact that it tends to be a temporary issue. Anyone can shit, snort, and blaspheme. Anyone can react without thinking, either on your own or in a crowd. It's the ones who adapt and overcome who will eventually lead us out of the chaos. Don't look at me—I don't want the job. But if you all turn around and run, you'll find me leading you after all because I'll be bringing up the rear.

CHAPTER 11

AFTER THE BASTARDS GO HOME

So . . . what have we learned today? More to the point: What have you learned, besides the fact that I'm a misanthropic cunt lip? I suppose I should apologize to you for learning something, if in fact that's the case. Then again, if you're going to write a book calling everyone morons, your ultimate goal should be to burn off the murky fogs of our reason. I'm not sure I did that, but I cursed a lot, told some stories, made some points, and did my best to hold up a mirror that in fact goes both ways. However, even though I really hope you have enjoyed this book, I am going to pretend that you have learned *nothing*.

As I'm fond of saying: you can call me Mike Hammer because I fucking *nailed* it.

Sadly it's true. We used to strive for greater things, to reach for the sky and stars. Now we barely clear arm's length. The only time we reach for the sky is when we're being arrested or held up—usually by someone we *know*. We scrape by on half way and take what we can get. Apparently these days aspirations are for pussies. That's no way to revolutionize a generation. It's shit like this that makes me want to mount the old War Cow and ride into battle with my wiffle ball bat that's riddled with spikes and nails, swinging like Skeletor on a feener.

The fucked-up thing is that we're in danger of passing it down to our children. Even if it feels like we're slowly phasing racism out, that doesn't mean it's our only dumb familial keepsake. We're all dumb in different ways, like rules and laws. In Michigan, schools will not allow children to bring peanut butter and jelly sandwiches for lunch. Why? Because of allergies—other children's allergies, as if the kids are using these sandwiches as weapons against those afflicted. If you're bringing PB&J to school, you might be a poor kid. You're not going to risk your meal on a kid who's equipped with an EpiPen. Ain't just the UP: kids in Vegas schools aren't allowed to bring backpacks to school. Why? Because of drugs. Because we *all know* every kid in the world is on fucking drugs. Kids have an excuse—they don't know any fucking better. All you adults? You guys are bulbous spitting dickheads, and you should fucking know better. The fact that you don't means the Mayans won.

I hate to say it, but a lot of this idiocy starts here in America—the "greatest" country on the planet, or at least that's what we're all so quick to say. I think we have to say that legally now. I believe some genius trademarked "the greatest country in the world" along with any and every variation of that statement and now gets half a penny whenever someone uses it in a speech or during a comedy show and so forth. The money from that phrase goes to cleaning the acid rain damage off of all of our national monuments. Pretty soon you'll see it on gag Ts in Camden, right next to "YOLO" and "Just Do It." That pretty much says it all, because once you've made it to those shitty T-shirts, your life as a piece of intelligence is very over. Just look how many people try to spread sage advice using thoughts like "Lead, follow, or get out of the way" and "No fat chicks." You're absolutely right, Brandon: *nobody* uses those phrases to appear smart. You know why? Because clichés are the quickest way to piss on the fires of intellectual thirst. With regret, no one pisses quite like America.

I've reached the age now that I would offer this country the same advice I give my friends and kids, and forgive me if I use one of those clichés I spoke about: actions speak louder than words. You can talk a great game, but if you don't back it up, all you're doing is hogging the oxygen and lying. I used to get pissed when people talked shit about America. Now I just duck my head and try to ignore the dumb shit, which means I tend to keep my head down all the time. All you have to do is look at our very strange sense of sexuality to determine that there's something very warped about these United States. We've gone from a people who once made Benny Goodman a sex symbol to peddling fuck tapes by the latest castoff from *Survivor*. Even my son has a weird sense of what it means to be from around here. He said something funny once and I told him he should be a comedian. He looked at me deadly serious and said, "I'm not a comedian. I'm a 'Murican." Besides the accidental profundity, the gallant little maniac had a point.

The crazy thing about my son is he's accidentally profound all the time. *So* much so that I wrote the stuff down for posterity. He likes to play outside in his camouflage costume a lot, so he'll paint his face to match it and splatter himself with fake blood left over from Halloween. After he's done, it takes hours to get the shit off, that's how covered he is. So after the first pass with the soap and water, I make him come out to show me. One time he hadn't quite gotten the fake blood all the way off and I told him he needed to go back because he missed some. He looked at me in shock and said, "Wait—you can still see the murder on me?" It gives me peace and shows me that deep down he knows what's up. I don't worry about video game violence and all that other "parent panic" shit with him; between his reservoirs of empathy and his burgeoning wit, he's going to be just fine. But other adults would throw a fucking tizzy. They have no relationship with their kids, so they don't talk. If they don't talk, they won't listen. So why would they listen when you tell them to get off their phones or computers and go outside? With a roll of their eyes, they just leave the room so you can't see them.

Oh my fucking god, speaking of phones and zoning out, I've got to tell you about a beautiful moment before I forget—classic fucking human behavior.

I drive a lot. Making the new Slipknot album, I had to drive in California a lot, which is like going in for a fucking enema every other day. When I drive, I pay attention, which means I watch people all the time. I watch people wander out into traffic to cross the street whether they're on the corner or not, and they're always on their phones, staring at the screen. Whenever I see people not paying attention to their surroundings and completely glued to their shitty little life suckers, my toe unconsciously inches toward the gas pedal. That's how ferocious I get. But this wasn't the case. But it was. Shit, let me explain a little better.

I was at the corner of Pico and Doheny, preparing to make a left turn—not a California Left, which means you drive for ten miles in the right-hand lane, then decide to cross two to three lanes of traffic in half a block when you get to the street you were looking for to make a left turn, yelling at people when they don't let you swerve right through their lives. No, I was going to make a proper left turn, which meant I got into the far lane miles before, used the turning lane *and* my blinker, and was waiting patiently for the gap in the traffic. I was sitting there, getting ready to make my move, when I saw a young man in what I can only describe as "Department Store Cool" clothes: pink V-neck scrubby T-shirt, khaki pants rolled right to below the knee, dress shoes, no socks, and a flip-brim hat with shitty graffiti underneath. Of course, he crossed the street slowly, staring at his phone the whole way, breaking at least two of my commandments in this very book. My knuckles whitened, my teeth grit, and I smoked my cigarette a little harder as I tracked his movements.

I'm here to tell you: I have a serious condition. You're reading the ramblings of a man with terrible anger issues. I say this because I was wishing and praying for something to happen to him the whole time I was watching him. I don't use the term "pray" very lightly—you all know me—but I tell you, I was almost willing to give in and subscribe to a faith *and* acquiesce to a deity as long as something shitty happened to this walking nightmare of an Old Navy commercial. Then suddenly a miracle happened. This kid's shoe snagged on a piece of the sidewalk that was jutting up and he fell so hard on his face that it looked like it hurt. I was so startled to have my wish come true that I laughed out loud—*really loud*, like loud enough the fucking kid heard me over whatever shit music was blaring in his ear buds. Hell, I didn't give a shit—I gave him the same smile I give everyone: "Serves you fucking right, you dickhead. Next time pay the fuck attention." It was then that I realized that my prayer had come true. A deal's a deal—I was fully ready to find a church and submit. I was, that is, until my own toe caught on the lip of a sidewalk while I was jogging, and I too went down hard. The universe had spoken: shit will happen everywhere.

Mea culpa, Old Navy Dude.

The world's fashion is fishing for what's new instead of what's awesome. No one gives a shit about feeling good as long as you've never felt it before, even though if you're old enough, you *have* felt it before. All they're doing is recycling the styles from twenty to thirty years ago. We do the same thing with music because lazy artists assume that people have no memory of the songs from the past, even though most of them are on a lot of the oldies stations. Laterally, designers automatically assume that you've forgotten style if you're old. Same shit—different decade. It's all recycling, as I've said. Also, the rule of thumb used to be "when comfort outweighs cool in regards to fashion, you know you're officially old." Now? Doesn't work or look like that. People from all walks of life dress like they're going down to pick up food stamps. Having grown up on food stamps myself, I know the look too well. I spent the first fifteen years of my life dressed as a "hipster"—now you want me to pay thousands of dollars to do it again? You can violently go fuck yourself.

I'm trying, kids. I'm really trying to understand why you do the things you do. Maybe it's the confusion that comes with age. The prior generation never understands the decisions of the one that follows it, and vice versa. But by now I've learned a few things. I've learned that if you're dreaming and your "character" has to pee, it means you're either going to wake up and rage-piss at 3 a.m. or you're going to wet the bed, the latter happening if your dream-self finds a bathroom. I've also learned this: life is like the statue in the stone—you have to grind away the shit that doesn't matter to see it, which is almost always made of the stuff between you and what you want on the inside. Yeah, I say and do a lot of crazy shit, but I've never let my eyes slip from what's important. God knows I've had plenty of opportunities to lose the map, the plot, and the place in the book. The fact that I'm still on the path means I'm doing something right.

Sure, I've made some enemies. The more I look around, the more it seems they're online too. There have been rumors of my death for years now. I'm beginning to think my main job in life is to piss people off with Wi-Fi. That's a lot of death-wishful thinking going on for that many rumors to start. They say "don't kill the messenger." That's all I am—a messenger. My message may suck and sting from time to time. But all it is, really, is offered advice. You could all tell me to go fuck myself in the end (not you wonderfully intelligent peeps reading this, of course, but those other people, the cattle with Instagram accounts . . .). If I spent half the time worrying about what people would say about me, I'd be a mute motherfucker with murder in his eyes. So I don't sweat it. I just get it. It's not my fault there are a lot of dumb-ass jive pricks on the ground. Then again, conversely, it's my right—and subsequent duty—to inform you when you all start to act like kack. Will it do me any good? Probably not. However, you don't run a marathon to get somewhere—that's why we have cars. You don't scream righteous indignation to hear yourself curse; you do it in the hopes that you might be heard someday.

Humans dress like shit, drive like shit, fly like shit, wait like shit, love like shit, talk like shit, act like shit, listen to shit, dance to shit, jump at shit, laugh at shit, make up shit, break up shit, and absolutely positively *take no shit* for it. We rub each other the wrong way, then fight to prove we're no "bitch" or that we're "keeping it real" or just being "straight thug." Is this all we got? Is this all that's left? A professional shit-throwing contest in which whoever still has clothing showing wins? Are we doomed to kill each other because we're all so stupid we don't understand the concept of "we're all in this together"? Will we ourselves be the reason that Homo sapiens die out like the other hundred variations of humanity that we eventually outlasted? Just the fact that I *know* some of you snickered at "Homo sapiens" doesn't exactly fill me with confidence for our future; in fact, it makes me want to crawl under my bed and read Stephen King's *The Stand* until Armageddon comes to flush our toilet. Be careful with the gun you pull—the finger on the trigger may be your own, but the target might just be yourself.

Let me explain to you how fucked up and malicious I actually am.

Sometimes, on those rare occasions when I have some time to myself, I consider a sadistic and hilarious scenario. I think about making my way out to an abandoned house somewhere, someplace quiet, remote, and dark. Picture that road that no one likes to go down. Now picture that house out there that no one wants to go to. Anyway, I'd go into that house, then I would sit cross-legged in the middle of one of the most removed of the rooms, the one at the very back corner or the one at the other end of the stairs. I would find that room, sit down . . . and wait. I would sit through the last of the day's light, watch the coming dusk, and let the resulting darkness wash over me like an effervescence. I would sit and wait . . . for someone to come around exploring. I know from experience that kids can't resist an abandoned *anything*. So I would just bide my time until someone showed up. It might not happen right away—hell, it might not even happen that night. It might take a couple of trips. But when someone did, I'd sit in the dark, listening to them move through the house. I'd wait until they got to the room I was sitting in.

Then I would scare the ever-living fuck out of them.

I would control my breathing as best I could, wait until they were well inside the confines of our surroundings, then I would simply say, "This isn't your house." Or I would just reach out one hand and tickle their ankle. Or I would move fast and push my nose against their face, whispering harshly, "You're not sup-posed to be here, motherfucker." Oh Mylanta, it would be divine torture. Then I would try to watch—as best as my eyes would allow me, having adjusted to the dark—and listen intently as they nearly killed themselves getting the fuck out of there. In a perfect world they would spread the word about "the insane dude who sits in the dark waiting for victims at that abandoned place over off the highway." That would then become an urban legend. Eventually I would have a hook for a hand, an eye patch, a wooden leg, and blood in my teeth. I would end up armed with a cricket bat lined with razor blades and a vicious backhand. Just thinking about it makes me smile until my face hurts. Then you know what I'd do? I'd wait until the scuttlebutt died down a little bit, then I would do the exact same thing, but this time dressed exactly like how the legend says I was dressed: hook, peg leg, eye patch, cricket bat, and a mouthful of fake blood, ready to scare bitches straight.

I wouldn't do this completely for myself. I'd do it to make a point. I read your posts, I watch your habits, and I have come to the conclusion that none of you are capable of handling the unexpected. You couldn't handle having the fuck scared out of you in a house you just assume is empty. So how are you going to handle rent, a mortgage, kids, bills, and so on? Basically, how are you going to handle life in general? I know according to that shitty fuckhole of a machine called television, every commer-cial and show makes life look like one big fucking Dairy Queen orgy, complete with acoustic jams and barbeques on resurfaced decks. This is not the case. You can't live with your parents for-ever, no matter how many times you drop out of school or lose your job at Claire's Boutique. You can't pay your bills or make a living if you fuck around your whole shitty life. What are you contributing to the world? If you don't have an answer for that, you aren't doing shit. You can blame everyone—politicians, musicians, teachers, actors, friends, and parents—all you want. But it's your shit. If it ain't together, you're fucked.

I know what you're thinking, and I completely concur. This is indeed my Angry Old Man book. That's okay. I went through the same stuff when I was your age. Sure, I lived with my Gram off and on for a long time after being kicked out of school and living on the streets—she was my savior. But I always had a goal in mind: music. I got to the point at which I could make a bit of cash at it even before I got signed with Slipknot. I had a job for rent and shit, but I played gigs for myself. I had an eye on the prize, and I never let that get away from me. Nobody has a prize anymore. All they want to do is have fun, be with their friends, and do stupid shit. How do you know you're having fun if you have nothing to compare it to when all you do is fuck off? And don't give me that teenager shit that "no one understands me." Of course they don't: you're a teenager. That is by definition the state in which you do your very best *not* to be understood and thereby never understand anyone in return. Granted, there are teenagers out there living incredibly brutal lives and yet somehow they keep it together because priorities are real. So not being understood is low man on the totem, right above giving a shit whether One Direction stay together and go the distance. You really want to be understood? Take a minute and pitch in; we might stop and give you a chance to vent.

It's a confusing fucking time in the world today. People still hate as much for color and twice as much for creed. They kill each other for gods they've never met. They hurt their women according to books written by those who might not have known any better. They hate based on biased faith instead of understanding based on accessible fact. I'm no better; you're no better. We're none the better until we try to do something about it. Until we put down the smartphones making us dumber and do something that has nothing to do with ourselves, we have a snowball's chance in an oven of achieving anything tangible in our lifetimes. The shit we do today makes as much sense as adopting an untamed baby puma. Sure, it bundles security, wanting a pet, rodent control, and exercise motivation into one nice furry switchblade package. But that's dumb. Anything that will eat your face whether you're alive or dead is not a good choice to have roaming around your house while you sleep. I think that metaphor says it all.

It's not just the young who are in danger of stepping on their own dicks, male or female alike. Oh no—this is not an isolated incident. I have several acquaintances who I've known for several years now—I say "acquaintances" because they give me gas, rash, and nothing but headaches. They're older than me but act just a shade older than my daughter, Angie, who turned twenty-two recently. They have kids but don't give a shit. They run in and out of "relationships" and look like an utter dick lip doing it—like, not even a boner either. At least a boner has a use. They make themselves look like the infected lip of a flaccid penis, only good for peeing if it ain't spitting stones. The thing is, they're so fucking oblivious to their own sucky state that they preen around "peacocking" like a dildo that sprouted legs. This is what thirty years of no responsibility looks like: their kids are older than they are, but their boyfriends and girlfriends never will be. It used to make me angry and embarrassed of them. Now I just avoid them like a pube on top of a urinal cake.

Once again the devil may be in the details, but the minutia is where the monotony lies.

Like I said before, I'm just as guilty of the cognizant atrocities I've described in this book. I guess one of my worst habits has to be constantly using the phrase "nobody gives a shit . . . " for this or that, in context with popular entertainment in our culture or anything else currently on the radars of the zeitgeist. But that's incorrect, isn't it? Because obviously someone or something *does* give a shit—that's why there appears to be so much focus on trivial clutter. I immediately assume people have the same state of mind and taste as myself, so I fling around definitive judgments like a discus thrower trying to qualify for the next Olympic trials. I'm an unapologetic asshole—this is what me and my kind do in the face of change or exasperation. So I suppose I need to check my shit. I need to think a little quicker on my feet before my mouth runs away with itself. I need to use the phrase "nobody *should* give a shit . . . " about this or that, because that's what I mean. That's what I hope. It's never true, but I tend to trend on the more hopeful side of possibility, contrary to what my street cred and Wikipedia says.

It may just be a case of this: reality is really just a reflected dimension of who we are as people. Maybe the music sucks and our driving sucks and our clothing sucks and our habits suck and our manners suck and our intelligence sucks and our relationships suck and our love sucks because . . . WE SUCK. God, could it really just be that simple? Everything sucks because we suck. We have all lost potential and gone coast to coast on a genetic road trip toward the barren wastelands of wasted space and cell deterioration. We're mental flunkies who can't pass the physical. So . . . does that make this book a moot point? Does this mean I just wiped my ass with however many pages and words in a futile attempt to get past the garbage dump only to realize this road only goes to the cemetery? Have we peaked in the past, making the future into nothing but a foreboding foregone conclusion? Is there anything worse than a paragraph that stretches just a little too long and is loaded with a ton of rhetorical questions that have no way of being answered right away? Can you see up my nose? Do I have a boog hangin'?

As a self-professed "negative moose knuckle," I have to proceed based on the facts at hand, which is to say that everything is going wrong and no one can agree on the right way to get back on track. As an "author," I have a sort of masochistic need for these calamities, for things to continue down the current path of destruction, because it provides me ample fodder for shit to write and rant about—in other words, your stupidity keeps me in business. But inside, deep down where I know no one can see or reach me, I *have* to believe things can get better. I cannot allow myself to descend to the depths of this hellish pragmatism that we as a species will never get back to a point at which we innovate instead of inundate with painful dumbness, that we as a whole will cut ourselves into halves then cut those into quarters just to prove the point that we can. At some point it has to stop just being the case of going against the grain to show the world we exist. We *know* you exist; we're looking at your stupid fucking pants and face. But it's not enough to exist; if we plan on getting together on another planet in a thousand years, we have to learn how to *coexist*.

That means thinking about others a little more often and thinking about yourselves a little less. *That* is what's really making me hate you the most. You're all in your bubbles, obsessed with what *you* need *right this second*. You're all shoved so far up your own asses you can get a good look at last night's gluten-free faux-turkey grinder sandwiches. You're all so busy typing away on message boards and social sites that you forget that not everyone needs to hear your pathetic excuse for an opinion every second of every day. You're all so glued to your phones, tablets, and computers that life isn't even running away from you at this point; it's strolling, taking its own sweet time because it knows damn well you're not going to pull your nose out of your Facebook page long enough to realize it's already gone. It has plenty of time to slip by in the night, making every morning blue and every second left just another countdown to the buzzer. Why the fuck should life wait for you? You've ignored it every chance you get.

You squander chances to celebrate by looking for the best way to tear the party down. You heap praise on subpar personalities while truly gifted talents waste away in obscurity. You flounder in the face of challenge because you've never had to think or fend for yourself in real life. You take advantage of every loophole and exit clause in the book. You change direction when it suits you and barrel into opportunity when you're not wanted. You act as if whatever is going on *right this second* is the most important thing in the world, even if it means you ignore what's on the horizon and never get past your myopic sense of right, wrong, and history. You're all just a bunch of fucking mayflies, living for a day, caught in the moment, only really interested in what the world can do for you, not what you can do for the world. You know what the "great" thing about being a mayfly is?

Nothing.

You can write down their achievements on the back of a matchbook and still have enough room for a grocery list.

There comes a time in a person's life when they have to find out what the future has in store. That used to be an exciting time for people: it meant they could relax just a little as they headed into the distance with the thrill of the hunt and a sense of direction. But it seems that in the last ten years the young are terrified of the future unless it has to do with social gatherings and gala events. Now, some of this anxiety may be because it seems like there's not a lot of chances to succeed out there. But

I think that for the most part people are just plain daunted by the looming specter of . . . responsibility. It freaks people out to think they will be shackled to a decision or a role for the better part of their lives. So they drive themselves to distraction with bullshit. Listen: if you have no responsibility, you have no room to grow or develop any sense of character. Character means not only who you are but also who you can be when the shit hits the fan. If you have no responsibility, you have no character. You're just a kid in grownup clothes. Sorry if that's a bit harsh, but it's true. I know it's true because I lived it.

I ran through life like a child through a sprinkler, throwing caution to the wind, never really bothered about anyone but myself for the better part of the first thirty years of my life. I broke people's hearts and destroyed people's trust. I took way more than I gave, including giving a shit about the damage I was doing. I hurt my friends. I never knew my eldest daughter until she was eleven. I was a horribly selfish person—talented, driven, angry, intelligent, and yet so narcissistic that I couldn't see through the haze enough to realize that none of my friends trusted me, none of my family took me seriously, and no one I worked with could rely on me for anything. Sure, when it came to what I wanted or needed to do, I was all about it, throwing myself into the work with a frenzy and a concentration that bordered on manic. But if it was outside my range of motion or vision, I could only really muster a passing nonchalance toward helping or giving a good goddamn.

Life has a way of shaking the shit out of you—right out of your head, right out of your mouth, right out of your body. It will shake you like a shark, grinding the grist to shreds in the pressure and cut of its teeth. Life has no need for you, you see. Life goes on with or without you. So it would only stand to reason that if you don't take up the fight, it will leave you as a casualty.

You want to know what the secret is? I figured it out, you know. I figured it out a long time ago. It was so simple that I can't believe it took me that long. You know what it is?

It's all about nudcnienoNJWV.

Sorry, my finger got stuck.

So what's the fucking moral of *this* goddamn book? "Everything sucks, so fuck it"? "Your music makes my balls drop"? "Dipshits should be forced to take busses, not planes"? "Movie nachos are *still* not real nachos"? "Honey Boo Boo's so bad, she makes me miss Snooki"? I could do this for a while. I often get stuck in these loops and find it very hard to get myself out sometimes. This is the price of hours spent picking up weird crumbs that are tumbling around my head and throwing them up in word form onto fake paper. Side effects may include rambling, runny nose, upset navel, Pica, incessant scratching, dizziness, and flared nostrils. Anyone who experiences these symptoms longer than forty years should definitely see a doctor . . . or a shrink . . . or at least talk to one of the dudes who spin the signs on Hollywood Boulevard—you know, the big arrows that say, "Gigantic Sale! Come On In!" Those guys are like wizards with those things! Some of them are hacks, of course, but that's because they never had the *training*! They never had the proper *training*! How are you supposed to twirl those things so effortlessly if you don't have the *training*? It's a goddamn *skill*! Skill takes *TRAINING*!

Yeah, even I don't know what happened there . . .

The moral. That's a little harder to find here than in my other books.

With *Sins*, it was all about getting people to ease back on their guilt, to cut themselves some slack. With *Heaven*, I wanted to answer my own questions about spirits and make myself feel a little better, that I'm not crazy. With this one? Christ, that's murky. I've often heard that "dumb don't wash off." If only it were that simple, we could run the whole planet through a few million car washes and be done with these shenanigans. But the cold fact is that we are a global, multicultural, rainbow-hued tribe of fucking dicks. We have no chance to stop being this way because, quite frankly, we are worse than dumb—we're incompetent. Incompetent people don't know they're incompetent. They just blithely blunder through their day-to-day with no care for any damage that happens in their wakes. When the mishaps are pointed out, they see the issue but don't do anything to adjust and fix their ways. Why would they? It didn't occur to them that what they were doing was wrong to begin with, so why would it occur to them to figure out what the right way would be to avoid another confrontation altogether?

We don't behave very well in public anymore; between snatch selfies in clubs and young ignorant cunts playing something as obscene as the Knockout Game, it's no wonder more and more fairly intelligent people are "living" through *Second Life*. When we do go out in public and, perish the thought *travel*, we fly like we've been drugged and act like Justin Bieber demanding free entrance into Disneyland at 1 a.m. People in airports are as vacuous as patients after med check and minutes before bedtime. Whether we're out and about or walking around our houses in private, we only really have two looks to go by: uncomfortably hip or just woke up. For us, it's either suave couture or sweatpants central. We're either going out on the town or in to the DMV to renew our fucking tags. You know where we find that in-between place, where comfort and decency come together a little closely? Ironically, it's simple: when we're older and we've stopped giving a shit, one way or the other.

When we drive we're in a constant state of either Schumacher or shmuck, dodging traffic while texting or sucking off our significant others—anything besides paying attention to the road ahead. In that way we drive a lot like we live. Seeing a pattern? It's pathetic, but not nearly as pathetic as what we spend our money on: the latest crazes for the earliest phases, ready and willing to take our minds off the fact that maybe we put too much emphasis on how much money you do or don't have to begin with. Some of that pressure, of course, comes from our families or our wives/husbands or our boy/girlfriends or our regular J-11 friends or society in general, putting more strain on already impossible relationships and steering that ship toward oblivion . . . or green Jell-O. Because we can't get our relationships together, we can't get our kids to keep it together. They're turning feral and, indeed, turning on each other. The abuse is starting younger and younger, to the point at which they'll need to start holding Bullying Seminars at Lamaze classes. Because we're getting dumber and dumber, our music—and taste thereof—is getting shittier and shittier. Which came first: the ass or the twerk? I really, *really*, *REALLY* fucking hope it remains a mystery to me.

Speaking of which, it's still a mystery as to why I am just as dumb today as I was before I was filling my own pants with the Brown Sound. Even though there are still times when the tiniest hint of the "underwear parentheses" finds a way to appear (shut up . . .), I consider myself a savvy cat with a handle on the times and places. But just when I think that, I walk head first into a door because I wasn't wide enough awake, or I piss on my brand-new Dalek socks because I always think I'm smarter than I actually am and decide I can go pee in complete darkness and be perfectly fine. I *know* for a fact that spicy food absolutely destroys my stomach, and yet I eat vast quantities of it, only to suffer the consequences in stunned disbelief. Yeah . . . if this is what a so-called genius looks like, I can only speculate how many times Einstein went sissy on his bedroom slippers. Trust me: I'm no Einstein. But I know my way around it.

So, for the most part, why are we all so fucking stupid?

Maybe it's a part of our DNA. Maybe it's a countdown of sorts. Maybe, if ancient astronaut theorists are to be believed (I just want to work that phrase into every book I write from now on), maybe when we were being groomed and grown by the Thetans (that's a nod toward those kooky Scientologists) or other aliens that may have been involved, they installed a fail-safe. See, I've seen a lot of movies and read a lot of big, thick, smarty-pants books. I know that if you're going to create a new version of life, a version that can learn and excel at leaps and bounds, you don't do it without making damn sure that it can't get too big for its own britches, whereupon it would rise up against its creators. That wouldn't make for a very nice Father's Day. No, no—the creators couldn't have that. So they put in a "safety valve" of sorts.

Maybe they installed in us this fail-safe that would kick in once we hit a certain capacity for intelligence and violence. Knowing that one could very well feed the other, once we'd peaked as a sentient species, the time would come for us to be devolved as one giant genus. Much like a cell that can be programmed to break down with the right stimuli, we humans could have been predisposed to a monumental trigger, ready to go off if our intellect became a threat beyond our own solar system. In order to protect themselves from these crazy mammals they'd helped to make rampant and reproduce, the alien uberlords would develop a way for that trigger to go off without their own interference being discovered.

A trigger like, say, splitting the atom?

That's a nice story, and for fuck's sake, I'd laugh my balls off if it were true. Then again, it doesn't change the fact that 99.99999 percent of the population is a heaping mass of messy headcheese, nearly as smart as the average pet rock. I see it all the time. Worse yet, I have to wade through it just to live a life that doesn't involve a cave, a gun, and a lot of "get off my lawn." I might be more angry if I didn't smell the same pheromones coming from my own neuro pits. To quote anyone who ever saw M. Night Shamalama-Ding Dong's movie *The Happening* . . . is that *it*? That's fucking *IT*?

Someday—and when I say *someday* I really mean most likely not in my lifetime—maybe we'll right this ship of fools and seek out smoother waters, cooler breezes, and better climes. That day isn't too far-fetched to dream about; life doesn't have to be fucking rocket science, and being able to think and act like better human beings isn't too much to hope for. Natural selection could easily come knockin' on our front doors with a warrant to besmirch the premises. But I tell you one thing: we may be dumb, but, motherfucker, we are *stubborn*. All it would take is for some force of nature to attack us, thinking we're too stupid to care or defend ourselves, and BAM! We'd kick ourselves into PhD mode just to prove a point. We are obstinate, cocky, committed killers when we want to be, and if we need to do some of that there "fancy book learnin'" to keep the wolves at bay, we'll fucking do it with relish (mainly mustard and ketchup, but also some relish).

Me? Well, if I live to see the troglodytes rise, I'll make peace with this warrior asshole who has it out for civilization—hell, I might even have forgiven you by then. I do know that even though you are truly making me hate you, my evil passion won't sustain itself very long. I totes heart chew guys (that sentence was for the younger kids). But until that glorious day I'll just go on hating you, as my tired bare feet seek out the warmer stones, my eyes adjust to squinting all the time, and, in the quiet of the midday sun, I calmly wait for that genetic alien bomb in my head to go off, putting myself and all of you out of my misery.

Thanks for reading.

My name's Corey Taylor.

Go home and fuck yourself.

ACKNOWLEDGMENTS

As always, there are so many people to thank and only so many fingers to count on, but I'll give it a go, nonetheless! First off, my wonderful group of "Archetype Acolytes": Uncle Tony, Brian and Casey, Dacia and Jimmy, my sister Jackie and those DAMN kids, Pam (Pand?), Sam (Sand?), The Band (The Bam?)—Jared, Bear Arms Drew, Andrew and Bruno, and, of course, Lady of the Face. You guys were all supertroopers! My buddy Strati Hovartos for the amazing photos; my sister Christine for making sure we looked great in said photos; Ben Schafer, Amber Morris, and everyone at Da Capo for their help and continued belief in me; Marc Gerald for getting me into this mess; Brennan, Diony, BoJo, Kimbo, and everyone at 5B (4B, 3B, and right on down the line); Gram and everyone else in my family—immediate, extended, and otherwise; the people of planet Earth who put the "Duh" in "Does this shirt make my ass look fat?"; last but not at all least . . . my wife, Stephanie, The Boss. I couldn't do any of this without you. Thank you for being my muse and my lucky charm. I love you so much.